DUCK
AND
(RE)COVER

DUCK

AND

(RE)COVER

The Embattled
Business Owner's Guide to
Survival and Growth

STEVEN S. LITTLE

WILEY

John Wiley & Sons, Inc.

For general information on our other products and services or for technical support, please contact our Customer Care Department within the United States at (800) 762-2974, outside the United States at (317) 572-3993 or fax (317) 572-4002.

Wiley also publishes its books in a variety of electronic formats. Some content that appears in print may not be available in electronic books. For more information about Wiley products, visit our web site at www.wiley.com.

ISBN 978-0-470-50490-1

Printed in the United States of America.

10 9 8 7 6 5 4 3 2 1

For my Father, Robert Palmer Little
(aka "Bob the Navigator")
who never steers me wrong.

Contents

Contents

DUCK

AND

(RE)COVER

Introduction

Stark Realities

All generalizations are false, including this one.
— Mark Twain

. . .

It was approximately 6:00 A.M. PST on October 14, 2008 when I discovered that a great many so-called experts had been wrong. Allow me to explain in full, as the lesson learned here is one that you and I should never forget. Indeed, this one example represents the overriding lessons to be learned from this entire book.

Throughout 2008, the consensus among the press and the pundits was that we were either in, or would soon be entering, an economic recession. The warning signs were all in place: rising unemployment, falling consumer confidence, and aggressive interest rate reductions by the Federal Reserve. Home sales in the United States were stagnating and values were falling. By mid-2008, various polls indicated that a majority of American consumers believed we were in a recession, and a wide array of public and private sector reports concurred.

By October, the precipitous stock market meltdown left little doubt in my mind that things were getting uglier. Yet our nation's business owners weren't ready to use the r-word quite yet. Just prior to the 2008 election, many experts and economists were pointing to increasing business owner optimism as a sign of an overall bottoming out of the economy. The National Federation of Independent Business (NFIB) monthly index of owner optimism actually improved from August through October. I began to hear a decidedly upbeat attitude among business owners at the events where I was asked to speak. "This thing is going to be over before you know it" and "It's all just media hype" were common refrains.

I could not share their buoyant tone. In my mind, the likelihood that we were headed for a significant downturn seemed very real, based on the unprecedented nature of the financial collapse. Being a self-described business growth expert, I knew it was important for me to recognize that, after years of speaking and consulting on the subject of growth during an economic boom, I now needed to dust off some sage advice on recessions. I had certainly weathered a few myself, and it was time to help business owners and managers prepare for the gathering storm.

Luckily, I seemed to have some real answers for business owners, based on my own experiences and more than 20 years of study regarding what works and what does not. This would be the fourth downturn I'd been through, and I felt compelled to share the things I had learned.

One idea I was espousing seemed to garner a lot of attention. I suggested to anyone who would listen that it was a proven *fact* that maintaining your advertising budget through a downturn is one of the best ways to grow your business over the long term. Everyone seemed to agree with me (and congratulate me for my profound wisdom), and why wouldn't they? The idea makes a lot of sense.

The argument for maintaining your advertising budget in a downturn is compelling: Most of your competitors for customer mind-share will cut their marketing budgets, allowing you to stand out and thereby putting you in a better position to prosper when things get back to normal. Due to the laws of supply and demand, marketing communication costs often decrease in a recession, making your reach more efficient than it normally would be. Besides, a whole host of studies had proven this approach to be correct. Or so I thought.

October 2008 proved to be the busiest month I had ever experienced as a business speaker; I presented in 11 cities in just 15 days. My overall message of growth, coupled with a new focus on rules for a recession, was working. Audiences were engaged like never before. Apparently, I was really helping business leaders. I have to admit that I was feeling pretty good about my message.

But on the morning of October 14, I began to question that feeling.

The day began innocently enough. After having flown to the four corners of our continent for seemingly weeks on end, I caught a travel break. I had two events back-to-back in the greater Phoenix area, spaced one day apart. I was still on east coast time when I woke early on my day off to hear an economist on Bloomberg News posit negatively on the newly proposed federal bank bailout. I wasn't sure I had heard it all correctly. I quickly checked WSJ.com and found the following headline:

U.S. to Buy Stakes in Nation's Largest Banks

That article went on to explain that that the move "intertwines the banking sector with the federal government for years to come." After weeks of speculation, the genie was now out of the bottle. Were these United States of America, land of free markets and Adam Smith's principle of "the invisible hand," trying to become France? I didn't know exactly what it all meant (and I'm not sure that anyone really does to this day), but I did know, in that moment, that nothing would ever be the same after this. The time had come to question everything about business as usual in this country.

The first thing I did was to look through the presentation I had built for the following day. Was it all still true? Did I still believe what I was planning to say to a group of 300 business owners? My name, the presentation title, and the date were all accurate. My first couple of rules held true because, as we will later learn, they are irrefutable. The first point that made me think "better check this out" was my assertion that maintaining your advertising budget in a recession was a proven strategy. I knew it was a truism, but also thought it would be best to document the proof.

I had a vague recollection of what I needed to find in order to verify the assertion. A simple Google search (I believe my keywords were "advertising," "recession," "study," and "sales growth") helped me find the information I needed. Sifting through the seemingly endless pages of results, it was clear that my foggy memory had not failed me. McGraw-Hill Research Laboratory of Advertising Performance Report #5262 was cited by almost every one of my Google hits.

Eureka! Here was the proof! In the face of a financial world now turned upside down, could it be that the real world of industry and commerce still had some absolute truths on which we all could depend?

My mind quickly returned to 1986, when, as a junior account executive for a regional advertising agency, I had first read the then new report by the prestigious publishing giant McGraw-Hill. Now, here it was again, all these years later, allowing me and thousands of others to make the unequivocal case that maintaining advertising spending through a recession causes sales growth.

Yet, as I began to dig a little bit deeper that fateful morning, I realized there was one glaring problem. The report doesn't say that at all.

What does report #5262 really tell us? The first sentence of the study is both succinct and insightful.

. . . a McGraw-Hill Research Analysis of 600 industrial companies showed that business-to-business firms that maintained or increased their advertising expenditures throughout the 1981–1982 recession averaged significantly higher sales growth both during the recession and for the following three years than those that eliminated or decreased advertising.

How much sales growth? The report claims 256 percent greater sales growth for the aggressive advertisers by 1985. Wow! This is one powerful finding. So powerful that you can now find thousands of references to it, from peer reviewed academic journals to online business bloggers. Do your own search and see what I mean. I simply picked a random page number (say page 33) and looked at the links. You'll undoubtedly find a range of examples such as the following that cite the magical properties associated with report #5262.

- A New England radio station touting the report as proof of why their local clients should keep spending money with them.
- A public relations firm in the U.K. saying the report demonstrates the importance of all marketing communication efforts in a downturn.
- A freelance copywriter who specializes in promoting the arts citing the report as evidence of the need for orchestras and theater companies to spend more on marketing in this recession.

WHY MY CONCERN?

Let's start with the broadest and most important thing we can take away from all this. Our lesson centers on the importance of truly understanding cause and effect. For centuries, big thinkers from Socrates to Einstein have struggled with the notion that one action (the cause) can be proven to produce another action (the effect.) While I am far from being a philosopher or nuclear physicist, I have learned that proving causality is rarely as simple as it seems.

If you ever hope to achieve a specific outcome in your business, then logic dictates that you thoroughly understand what causes a desired effect. For example, we are looking closely at report #5262 and trying to better understand how it applies to you and your business. Yet this is simply one example being used to shed light on how easily prevailing wisdom can obscure your vision. The time has come for you to question these closely held beliefs in all aspects of your business, whether financial, operational, human resource management, and yes, advertising initiatives.

So, can we say for certain that maintaining or increasing advertising in a recession (the cause) results in significantly higher sales growth (the effect)? Near the end of report #5262, the professional researchers at McGraw-Hill provide us with an unambiguous answer to our all-important question: "This analysis does not permit any statement of causality."

The sentence is not set in fine print or hidden with an asterisk at the bottom of the report. In no uncertain terms, the researchers are saying that we cannot conclude that maintaining or increasing advertising in a recession causes sales growth. They are also saying that one cannot conclude that decreasing or eliminating advertising in a recession causes a company's sales to fall behind. Instead, they rightly pointed to a statistically significant correlation between advertising and sales growth. Yet, as anyone who has ever muscled through a statistics class knows, correlation does not imply causation.

See if you agree with my logic here. While it is impossible to look back and know for sure, I am willing to bet your annual advertising budget that the following statements are also true about those 600 businesses studied in the recession of 1981/82:

- Firms that maintained or increased their landscaping budgets in the recession experienced superior sales growth through 1985.
- Firms that maintained or increased their annual holiday party and Fourth of July picnic budgets in a recession experienced superior sales growth through 1985.
- Firms that maintained or increased their new office furniture budgets during the recession experienced superior sales growth through 1985.

I think you see where all of this is going. When entering a recession, companies that are doing well are in a better position to continue to do well. Firms that were already on shaky ground during good times are most likely to feel the adverse effects of a sudden downturn. Firms that are experiencing sustainable, profitable growth are more likely to be able to afford more comfortable office furniture. However, increased spending on new office furniture does not cause sales growth.

Besides the obvious problems regarding causality, a simple reading of the executive summary provides us with a host of other potential problems. Start with the fact that the study looked only at publicly-held entities. The average sales per company studied was over $1 billion a year, with average advertising expenditure per company greater than $40 million annually. Does that sound like your business? The study also concentrated on companies that had survived the recession. In other words, they had to have sales data in 1985 in order to be included. So by definition, everyone studied survived beyond the recession. How about this for a logical conclusion: It doesn't matter if you increase, decrease, or maintain your advertising budget . . . at least you'll survive!

If you own a relatively large industrial company with a business-to-business advertising bent, and you believe that understanding actions taken in the early 1980s might be useful in furthering your cause in the twenty-first century, then by all means, get this report and read it.

For the rest of us, it is important to recognize that the information in the study is simply not actionable. It is, at best, merely anecdotal information that has been inexcusably misused to support arguments that couldn't be further from the actual findings (through no fault of McGraw-Hill's, I might add).

What are some of your closely held beliefs about the best ways to navigate the choppy waters of a recession? Do you know for certain whether they are really true? Were they once true, but could they have lost relevance in this uncertain environment?

As the sun began to rise in Phoenix on the morning of October 14, 2008, I put all this together and realized that we had been wrong about far more important issues than just advertising. The experts on Wall Street had been wrong. The experts in Washington had been wrong. So too were thousands of self-proclaimed experts like me who, with nothing but the best of intentions, were guilty of citing a study that didn't actually say what everyone wanted to believe it said. It was time to question everything.

For an embattled business owner like you, the lesson of Report #5262 is simple: In a crisis, conventional wisdom often defies common sense.

Section I

Pressing Immediacies

The term "duck" can mean a lot of different things in different contexts. I want to be sure that any embattled business owner is clear on my use of the term here.

My father, an ex-Air Force man and present-day athlete, ends every phone conversation by telling me to "keep my head down." It's good advice; keeping your head down is one way to avoid trouble. By putting your head down you present a diminished profile and therefore a smaller target. Thinking about Dad's signoff in the context of this book, though, makes it take on an added meaning.

Business authors are accused of overusing sports analogies, but in this case they are the most effective way to explain what I mean by the word "duck." In nearly every kind of athletic activity, there is a ready position that requires you to duck. Baseball infielders crouch, lowering their center of gravity and preparing to react at the crack of the bat. Football linemen come into a three-point stance in anticipation of a pounce off the line. Boxers, golfers, wrestlers, sprinters, swimmers, tennis players, and martial arts combatants all duck in their own way. It puts them in the best position to release a focused, explosive movement when the time is right.

You should put your organization in a similar position right now in order to focus your potential energy. An effective duck now will enable you to apply that energy when it's really needed. I'm not talking about "ducking" as in cowering in fear, and I don't mean to retreat or assume a wholly defensive posture, either. You need to get your business in the ready position.

Think of ducking as your first, most immediate response to crisis. It's what you need to do—today, right now—in order to avoid the near and present dangers and to put yourself in the proper position to recover when that opportunity comes.

Chapter 1

What Is Your Reality?

Conventional wisdom tells us that there are many logical steps business owners can take to survive and eventually grow in an economic downturn. Common sense says you must start this journey at the beginning.

Whenever business owners have a problem for which they seek my advice, they are always very good at giving me pertinent information. They have a situation they have already pondered at great length and are therefore able to give me a very cogent, logical description of the salient issues and questions surrounding their vexing problem. Business owners value logic a lot.

In more than 20 years of advising owners and leaders of organizations, I've never had one tell me that part of the problem was his or her lack of logical thinking. Not once. Yet when I am allowed to dig a bit deeper into the specific issue, the owners' and leaders' lack of logical thinking is always a major contributing factor to the problem itself. *Always*. I mean every time, without fail.

My ability to see their faulty logic has nothing to do with how smart I am. In fact, more often than not, business owners are smarter than this so-called expert in many ways. They are certainly more knowledgeable about their specific business and industry. I would also guesstimate that many, if not most, have a higher mental aptitude than I do. While I have no data to support that contention, I know that I tend to gravitate toward really smart people. My brother, sister, and son are all off-the-charts smart, and therefore I am comfortable working with people who have better minds than mine.

No, I am not smarter, but I do have two things most business owners don't have: an outsider's perspective and a long history of pattern recognition. As an outsider, I don't carry any preconceived biases about the specific situation. As a practitioner, I have the knowledge that can only be gained from repetition. Business problems are rarely unique, and I see the same ones repeated again and again. For me, just as it is for a general practitioner (MD), extremely rare conditions are extremely rare. We both see the same basic problems on a daily basis, which over time makes us better at accurate diagnosis and effective treatment. Regardless of the initial symptoms, I treat illogical thinking more than any other malady.

All business leaders believe they are logical thinkers and actors. They are also very good at uncovering logic fallacies in others' thinking. Reams of research show this is simply human nature. Most people, regardless of intelligence and experience, fall victim to this paradox. We all have biases and blind spots, yet we are much better at seeing them in others than in ourselves. In my experience, this paradox holds even truer for business owners.

Let's face it. We all behave irrationally at times. When things are going well, there isn't much call for self-examination regarding your decision-making skills. You can get away with your unique quirks and predispositions. Those that surround you have no reason to rock the boat by pointing out your less-than-logical ways. Without any negative feedback, business owners who've had any success at all begin to believe they are immune to the dangers of faulty thinking. They're not. I'm not. You're not.

When a sudden crisis emerges, lack of logical thinking and an unconscious tendency to ignore a new reality become central issues for the embattled business owner. This book is filled with commonsense strategies, proven tactics, real-world advice, and core questions you need to consider in order to duck and recover. Yet this book will be of no use to you if your thoughts and actions aren't based on sound reasoning. The time has come for you to confront the notion that, in some significant way, your own self-imposed mind traps are holding you back. At the risk of offending you before I've even had a chance of guiding you, I am saying that the problem is you.

You are the primary reason the business has had any success to date. You are also the most likely potential barrier to growth. In most cases, you are all the good and all the bad in your organization. Sure, the economic environment is playing havoc with the world of industry and commerce. Of course you are facing unprecedented challenges, many beyond your immediate control. Yet a clear path to survival and growth is possible and it begins with you.

I don't know you (not yet anyway). I don't know where you need to look to find your own clarity. I do know how other owners and leaders get lost and perhaps you will recognize yourself in a few of these common missteps.

OVERCOMPENSATION IS YOUR ENEMY

As I write this, I am watching a small fishing boat navigate a narrow inlet to reach the open ocean. It is proceeding slowly and appears to be going straight ahead. I can't see who is steering, but obviously the captain has done it before, because the boat isn't in any danger of hitting the sides of the channel. The captain is no doubt steering with accurate, timely corrections in an effort to reach the ocean safely and efficiently. Experience is on his or her side.

At other times, I have watched this same inlet while an obvious newcomer to boating attempts to steer straight ahead. Despite their best attempts, such novices perform what amounts to a series of S-shaped maneuvers, narrowly averting the sides all the way through the passage.

What is happening to the novice is called overcompensation, resulting from delay in the system. The time between the turning of the wheel and the resulting change of direction is the delay. The inexperienced boater inadvertently produces wild fluctuations in direction, as he or she overcompensates due to lack of a timely feedback. New boaters turn the wheel but nothing happens immediately. Then they begin to panic and turn the wheel too much. Delay causes the beginner to function inefficiently and therefore dangerously. Overcompensation is the root cause and the true enemy.

The same phenomenon can be observed in embattled businesses. Lately, I've seen many owners blindsided by problems that they should have been monitoring all along. Once the situation has reached the level of a real crisis, it's difficult to take efficient corrective action. In an attempt to make up for lost time, owners often overcompensate. This only serves to further exacerbate the overall problem.

Taking corrective actions in your business will invariably result in some delayed responses. Remember, irrational overcompensation is your enemy, especially when you have a narrow margin for error.

STATUS QUO IS AN EQUAL FOE

Embattled business owners are presented with an ever-increasing number of difficult decisions. In good times, they take bold actions because they clearly see the potential rewards. They also tend to be much better at picking a specific course of action that is the best choice among other positive alternatives. However, when faced with the more troubling dilemma of picking among alternatives viewed as potentially negative, risky, or unpleasant, many choose to do what they have always done, or to do nothing at all. They stick with the status quo.

In some ways, this behavior is the opposite of over-compensation (doing too little versus doing too much). Yet these behaviors are actually very similar in the sense that they are both rooted in faulty thinking about risk, reward, and time. Both behaviors create an even greater potential for escalating problems in a crisis.

When faced with a number of risky alternatives with uncertain rewards, many owners put decisions off, hoping that more time (i.e. information) will make the decision easier. In some instances, that may be true. In many other scenarios, it is a tragic mistake. There are unquestionably moments when bold actions are not only the best alternative, they may be the only real alternative. Yet many leaders fail to act in a timely manner. Academics call this risk (or loss) aversion, and I see more evidence of it among business owners now then ever before.

Throughout this book you will be presented with specific areas that might need your immediate attention. Don't wait for more information or a return to normalcy when the alarm bells of a true emergency ring out. Problems can wait. Emergencies demand the best possible decision you can make at the moment.

If your largest customer has recently reneged on a big contract, the stark reality is you're being adversely affected because you allowed them to be your biggest customer. If the foot traffic in your mall has gone from bad to worse, recognize that you chose to remain in that location. If your top salesperson just left you, taking a few of your best customers with her, face the fact that you didn't make it attractive enough for her to want to stay. If your megabank that said they loved you a few years ago suddenly won't return your phone calls, know that a local or regional player may have been a better option all along.

In a crisis, it is only human nature to point the finger of blame away from ourselves. Is it fair that your town's largest employer just laid off 11,000 workers? No. Was it foreseeable? Maybe. Is it a stark reality? Absolutely.

This worldwide crisis of confidence all began with the collapse of U.S. residential real estate. The meltdown has not been uniform. In some markets, values have eroded 40+ percent, while other areas of the country have been relatively unaffected so far. In those areas where the bubble inflated the most, the burst appeared to happen suddenly and without warning. Now, looking back with 20/20 hindsight, the housing collapse shouldn't have surprised anyone paying attention to well-established fundamentals and historic norms.

I've spent a good bit of time in the greater Detroit area over the last few years. Each time I'm there I am struck by the resiliency of the people and the quality of life in many areas. Yet, due to game-changing market forces such as excess inventory levels, white-collar job losses, and stricter lending practices, luxury home building has all but stopped in Detroit. If you have differentiated yourself as the builder of choice for upscale homes in greater Detroit, you are truly embattled. Even if your business has been there for generations, you have to face the new stark reality. Building luxury homes in Detroit, Michigan, will not be a clear growth opportunity for the foreseeable future.

In this instance, business as usual is over now. If you are this embattled builder, you have to take bold and swift action just to stay afloat. You could remain in Detroit and fight it out in market segments where you have never competed. You could look to diversify into commercial building or remodeling. Or you could move to an area where your unique skills are more likely to be rewarded in the near future. There are growing markets in this country where luxury homes are more likely to be built over the next few years. The question becomes: Are you a Detroit builder or are you a luxury home builder? Either way, the choice is yours and only you can make it.

Conventional wisdom tells us that luxury homes won't be built in greater Detroit for many years. My common sense tells me that your best chance for survival and growth is to move your business to a burgeoning market. However, regardless of what I think, or what experts say, only you can make the right decision for you. More than a few intrepid luxury home builders will stay in Detroit and prosper over the long term. It won't be easy, but they will find a way to meet the market challenges (especially with fewer worthy competitors left standing). Others will take their expertise to growing markets where they have no contacts or suppliers and still carve out a profitable niche for themselves. Too many will do too little and simply won't make it.

YOU ARE YOUR ALLY

This book would be much easier to write if I could just tell you to ignore conventional wisdom and follow common sense (yours and mine). Unfortunately, nothing in business is ever that clear-cut. Indeed, if it were, your business wouldn't need you. You could simply put relevant data into some software program and allow it to make all your decisions. But your business does need you. Only you can ascertain which widespread beliefs and which of your own closely held convictions apply to your present circumstances.

Consider this example. Conventional wisdom says that business owners don't monitor their internal financials closely enough. Accountants, academics, and consultants all agree that not managing to obtain accurate and timely financial information is one of the primary causes of business failures. In this case, the conventional wisdom matches what I've experienced in working with privately held businesses. Most business owners are more interested in pursuing their passion than they are in immersing themselves in the box scores of their business. Here, conventional wisdom and common sense converge into one irrefutable truth: Your business can't win consistently if you don't know how to keep score.

Conventional wisdom also tells us that maintaining or increasing advertising in a recession leads to sales growth. However, common sense says, "It depends." There are too many other variables involved to make this one sweeping generalization applicable to you. My common sense, based on past experience in downturns, is that nimble, privately held businesses can grab market share from their paralyzed competitors by marketing more aggressively. I've done it, and I've seen others do it successfully. I've also witnessed desperate owners plow their dwindling resources into ill-advised and unsuccessful marketing initiatives that directly contribute to their ultimate demise.

I know you want answers. If you are embattled, you could be reading this book because you want me to tell you what to do. Yet it would be irresponsible of me to oversimplify complex issues. For example, should you increase, decrease, or maintain your marketing expenditures during this downturn? If you are a relatively cash-flush company serving a growing market segment, the answer is probably "increase." If you are a luxury home builder in Detroit, the answer may be "dramatically decrease." If you are a well-established business in a stable market, "maintain" might make the most sense.

No, embattled business owner, I can't tell you what to do. That responsibility lies solely on your shoulders. What I can do is point you toward those areas that most need your focused attention and efforts. I am recommending a two-pronged approach. This section of the book addresses the pressing immediacies (the *duck* phase) that will help ensure your survival and put you in a better position to seize the inevitable growth opportunities created by change, which is covered in the second section of the book (the *recover* phase). While business owners are the targeted readers, the guidance offered in these sections should apply to any leader in any organization that wants to, in effect, own any situation. From nonprofit principals to big business bosses, everyone wants to think and act more entrepreneurially these days. This book is intended to help you do that very thing.

Regardless of who you are, the problem is you, or at the very least your problems are yours. Before you can even hope to win the battles ahead, you must start with a personal reality check. What do you believe about your business that isn't true? What may still be true about your business, but fear has caused you now to question it? Is overconfidence skewing your judgment? Are you relying on gut instinct when unbiased information would serve you better? Is the dread of potential defeat impairing your effectiveness? Are you confident in your ability to cause desirable effects in a new world that often defies common sense?

As you consider the guidance offered in this book, re-member that your business's survival and growth depend upon your ongoing ability to accurately perceive your new realities. Don't fool yourself.

Chapter 2

Triage and Tourniquets

The term *triage* dates back to the Napoleonic wars and the battlefield practice of separating the wounded in order to prioritize time and resources.

Today, the use of triage has expanded beyond the battlefield to include disaster sites, emergency rooms, and so on. While there are various accepted protocols, most triage categories look something like these four:

1. **Immediate**—These patients are the highest priority and require immediate attention. They will not survive if they are not attended to quickly.
2. **Delayed**—This group requires medical attention within a few hours. Their traumas are potentially life-threatening, but they are stable enough to wait for care.
3. **Minimal**—These walking wounded can wait until higher-priority patients have been stabilized.
4. **Expectant**—This is the hard one. These patients have a low probability of survival, regardless of treatment. In other words, treating *expectant* patients would require withholding time and resources from those others who are more likely to survive.

Clearly, these types of decisions are gut-wrenching. Tagging a patient as expectant is likely to be a death sentence. Yet the trained expert understands that

decisions made in triage actually save lives. Dispassion-
ate logic is the key to successful triage. It requires emotional detachment, something that is difficult for almost
anyone.

Business triage also demands that you suppress your
ego and emotion. What can appear cold and calculating
is actually compassionate. In a crisis, the role of the leader
is to prioritize what can and should be saved. The overall
survival and growth of your business is in the interest of
your customers, community, employees, vendors, and yes,
yourself and your family. Everyone is depending on you
to make some tough decisions.

Can your business survive in your current location?
Can you truly afford the space you occupy now? Do you
have a pet project that should be tagged "expectant"? Is
there a loyal, long-term employee who has become part
of the problem and not the solution?

Like medical triage, business triage decisions are
made in the midst of a crisis. All the training and experience in the world won't eliminate errors in judgment.
Time is the critical resource in crisis management. The
necessity for snap judgments often causes even the most
experienced practitioners to make fatal errors.

Studies of emergency responders and medical professionals show that human beings are likely to err on the
side of *overtriage*. That is to say, they are likely to put too
much time and energy into trying to save a patient who is
beyond hope, or to concentrate on the walking wounded

patient in front of them at the expense of those in more dire need. The purpose of triage is to prioritize; clearly not everyone can be a top priority.

In my years of observing business owners in a crisis, they too are likely to overtriage those areas closest to them. Are you guilty of overtreatment in those areas of your business to which you have the most emotional attachment? Is that misdirected focus causing other, more critically injured but salvageable areas, to suffer?

At a time like this, every critical injury can appear as if it is potentially fatal. Hemorrhaging can be ugly, especially if you have never seen it before. You need to get your priorities in order.

Step back from your business and look for those areas that need your attention the most. Avoiding the common pitfalls discussed below should help you do that.

NOT FOCUSING ON ROOT CAUSES

Don't allow symptoms to distract you from treating the real trauma. For instance, if customer satisfaction is down, it doesn't necessarily mean you need to prioritize customer service training. Perhaps your inventory management system is the primary cause of the problem. A wholesaler's decision to suddenly stop shipping to a habitually slow-paying customer may appear to treat a cash crunch condition. Yet the true cause of the cash crisis may have very little to do with the customer's tardy behavior, and a hasty "cut-'em-off" decision may actually cause the customer to stop paying, making the condition worse.

NOT PRIORITIZING AREAS THAT NEED YOUR ATTENTION

Most business owners have a certain bent. In a crisis, we all have a tendency to prioritize whatever we know best, regardless of its current condition. For the owner with an engineering bent, everything appears to be an operational issue. For an owner with a sales bent, jamming more leads into the prospect funnel cures all ills. The owner who leans toward accounting honestly believes that endlessly tweaking budget spreadsheets is time well spent.

Whatever your bent, that area of expertise and comfort in your business is probably pretty well covered. Too often, it is the area you haven't paid attention to that needs your attention now.

NOT PUTTING NEW AND RECENT PROBLEMS IN PERSPECTIVE

If you've never had a threatening collection call, the first one can be jarring. For some business owners, however, a collector threatening to repossess their firstborn is just

another day at the office. We all have a tendency to over-
prioritize problems that are unique in our experience.
Whatever the crisis du jour is, be sure that you are able
to frame it properly. Is it really the most important thing
for you to address today, or is it simply the most unsettling
issue you've dealt with recently?

NOT KNOWING HOW TO APPLY TOURNIQUETS

As a young lifeguard I was certified by the Red Cross in
various methods of first aid. One of the most important
things I learned was the proper use of tourniquets. As you
probably know, a tourniquet is a constricting, bandage-
like device used to limit blood loss when a limb's artery
has been severed. I was always taught that the decision to
apply a tourniquet was a decision to lose a limb. A drastic
measure, but it sure beats losing a life.

When a business such as yours is in crisis, the owner
often has to make the difficult decision to cut off the
lifeblood of resources. In order to save the overall business, he might find it necessary to stop the bleeding within
an injured project, a department, a product launch, or an
underperforming location. You should understand that
in business, as in first aid, the decision to apply a tourniquet could cause you to lose that arm of your business
forever.

First aid has come a long way since my days as a lifeguard, however. New high-tech tourniquets have the potential to save not only lives, but limbs. The successful application of these new tools depends on expertise and experience. In business, it is also possible for an owner to temporarily stop the bleeding and regain the use of the limb later. Panicky entrepreneurs are notorious for applying pressure with crude constraints that fail to save anything. In which areas of your business do you have the experience and expertise to apply tourniquets? As you look for ways in which to stop the bleeding, remember that crudely applied devices can produce unintended and deleterious consequences.

Chapter 3

All Hail the Cash King

There is one nugget of conventional wisdom that you always hear about surviving a recession: "Cash is king." The question is, what does this mean? How does this axiom apply to you? Or does it apply to you?

There's no question that effectively managing cash flow is your first priority in a crisis, regardless of your cash position today. I'm willing to bet you have a much different relationship with cash now than you did a year ago. If, as an embattled business owner, you are feeling a cash crunch, you've already been forced into some corrective actions. Yet even if you are feeling pretty good about your bank balance and your projected pro forma, now is the time to anticipate a significant reversal of fortune.

We live in a time when the nation's pillars of industry and commerce have been brought to their knees. Unprecedented volatility in our nation's economy creates a certain uncertainty for you. While what you know is true may remain true, it is also more possible than ever that the prevailing winds of change are going to affect your business.

During good times, cash management seems to take care of itself. It's easy to take your eye off your financials when the economy is strong, steady, and running in your favor. Inefficiencies, waste, and pointless processes are somehow less apparent when you are in the money. In reality, a back-burner approach to fiscal oversight always

41

puts your business in danger of a cash management boil over. A recession only turns up the temperature.

It's no secret that the mishandling of cash is the most common cause of business failure. (In fact, other than voluntary closure or legal troubles, running out of money is the *only* reason businesses fail.) The question becomes: What causes businesses to run out of money? Obviously declining revenue (inflow) can be a key contributing factor in times like these. As a result, many owners are forced to improve their cash flow position through cost containment (outflow).

So here's my advice. Put together a cash flow projection for your business immediately. If you know how, go ahead and do it. If you don't know how, then find someone who does and get it done. If you already have a cash report, do it again and challenge your previous assumptions.

There's no need to try to project out too far when you're in the "duck" phase. For most business owners, a continuously monitored 90-day projection of anticipated revenue, costs, and collections will be of the most value. I suggest that erring on the side of caution is critical too. Many business owners are half-full optimists. In uncertain times, your projections should assume a few unwanted surprises.

There are a number of ways in which you can improve your cash flow by getting your hands on OPM (other people's money). Increasing profitable revenue—getting more money from your customers—is obviously one of them. Loans would be another. Banks and other financial institutions were falling all over each other trying to win your business when money was cheap and plentiful. Perhaps you've noticed they're not quite as interested in businesses like yours as they used to be, especially if you really need the money.

The traditional source of emergency funds has been family and friends. Chances are they're feeling far from flush these days. If you can't prove a plan for a home run idea and you're not willing to give up substantial ownership, angel investors and venture capitalists are probably not an option. Credit cards are an expensive way to stay afloat, and issuers are becoming more risk-averse every day. Loans secured by the Small Business Administration have dropped significantly and are in a state of unprecedented flux.

As some of the traditional cash wells have dried up, cost control becomes paramount. *Finding ways to better control how money is flowing out of your business is the one way to actively and quickly impact your cash position.* Here are some of the best places to start.

INDIRECT OVERHEAD COSTS

Every business has expenses that are not directly related to the product or service they offer. These can include everything from property maintenance to copy machine toner, from administrative staff to break room coffee service. These are often the first places businesses like yours look to cut costs and thereby conserve cash. I'm all for creative cost cutting. But I have seen some common pitfalls in this approach.

Many organizations tend to be penny wise and pound foolish when they start to cut costs. You should closely examine your largest overhead line items first and try to find ways to reduce them. Some organizations that need to seriously consider whether they even need an office may waste time arguing about comparatively inexpensive supplies for that office. I recently sat in a meeting with an owner and her five well-paid managers, who were considering ways to slash overhead. In terms of man-hours, the 20 minutes they spent debating the price/value relationship of various paper towel options was greater than any potential near-term savings.

When was the last time you viewed your current office equipment leasing agreement? Your company's liability insurance coverage? Your phone bill? These are examples of costly line items that need your scrutiny.

Leaders often fail to anticipate the unintended consequences of their cost-cutting actions. You may not notice the difference between temperatures of 72 and 68 degrees in your location, but will your best patrons still be comfortable? Customers may not tell you they are uncomfortable with your recent cost cutting measures; they may just not come back.

RENT

If you rent or lease any kind of space, now may be a great time to renegotiate. Renegotiation doesn't convey weakness. From a landlord's perspective, you may be a model tenant if you're making any payments at all right now. For landlords it's far easier to keep someone in a space than it is to find a new tenant. Ask your landlord to get creative.

If your current space is inadequate or too expensive and they're not willing to renegotiate, there are plenty of vacant spaces on the market. While there are dramatic differences by geography, many areas of the country are overbuilt with commercial real estate. This oversupply of space leads to potential savings for you. Although moving your business can be potentially disruptive, the cash saved in the long run may make the move worth it.

PAYABLES

When times get tough, everybody tries to stretch out their payments. Obviously, not paying your bills is a great way to conserve cash. However, there is little chance you can get away with it for any length of time and not suffer adverse effects. Besides, it's unethical.

In the real world, most vendors and debt holders monitor what you owe them pretty closely, especially in a recessionary period. What message does it send to your customers when you run out of a popular replacement part?

What does it say to your employees when the dumpster hasn't been emptied in more than a month? Juggling your payables can be a good trick, but be sure you understand which balls you can't afford to drop.

If you find yourself behind on your payables, do the right thing and communicate. Not only do the people you owe money to deserve to know what's happening, but it is in your best interest that they believe your intentions are honorable. Today, businesses of all sizes are struggling to pay their bills on time. Too many try to hide from their creditors by avoiding phone calls and ignoring e-mails and letters.

If you hope to minimize any potential damage to your existing relationships, be honest and open with those to whom you owe money. If you know you are going to be late, tell them. If you know when you can pay them, tell them that too. If you can provide them with a proposed payment schedule, it demonstrates a good faith effort.

The one ball you obviously can't afford to drop is your tax liability. Don't make the mistake of improving your cash position simply by holding off on tax payments. This is not a winning strategy!

RECEIVABLES

It probably comes as no surprise to learn that I recommend being especially vigilant regarding your receivables.

Closely tracking who owes you money is as important in good times as bad. Unfortunately, the importance of the collection process for many companies becomes a priority only after cash problems are painfully obvious.

If you have been keeping a close watch on your receivables all along, good for you. But many business owners overreact when collections get tougher. During good times the money is rolling in and customers who are habitual late payers are allowed to slide a little. As long as they're sending money in every month, nobody is particularly worried about which specific invoices are being covered. Once a cash crunch pressures an organization, too many owners make sweeping pronouncements: "I don't care who they are; if they are one day past due, I want you to cut them off!"

Here again, overcompensation is the enemy. By applying this particular tourniquet, do you risk losing a highly valued customer? One who is simply paying you the way you trained them to pay in the past? When you sic Bill or Betty the Bulldog on any customer in a reactionary attempt to raise cash, you risk scaring them off permanently.

My advice is that you treat each customer's situation individually. Every customer has a unique history with your organization, and you need to weigh the risk and reward of squeezing them for payment when they are cash-starved too. Your direct involvement with the largest and most important customers is critical. Often, lasting relationships can be forged when two organizations agree to help one another meet challenges like this together.

By the way, sometimes selling your receivables to a third party can be a way to generate cash. You can either use factoring services on the front end or a collection service on the back end. Both can make a lot of sense in certain circumstances. Given the turbulence in the financial services sector right now, be sure you shop these services carefully.

INVENTORY

Inventory management is complicated. In some businesses, such as distribution, inventory management *is* the business. In other businesses, people's time is the only inventory that matters. For many companies, inventory is the area that is most fraught with risk, yet it represents the greatest potential cash conservation reward.

When it comes to inventory control, the main thing is to control the *main things*. Every business I've known has had just a few main things. In your business, you have only a smattering of SKUs, a couple of menu items, or one specific service that matters the most. Don't make the mistake of micromanaging and thereby overcomplicating your entire inventory system. You know what sells. You know what you can never afford to be without. Never ever run out of your main things.

Too many business owners see specific inventory levels as a necessity. I see inventory as cash tied up in something someone else doesn't want right now. One could even argue that any inventory you are currently holding is due to your poor planning.

So how can you never run out of the main things and do it without inventory? You probably can't. The point is that we all need to see inventory for what it is: a place where free cash flow gets locked behind bars. Your goal should be 100 percent customer satisfaction with as little inventory investment as you can possibly manage. Don't accept the conventional wisdom in your industry regarding inventory levels. Common sense dictates that you alone have the information and experience to know what will work best for you.

Idle inventory is also your adversary. Clear out the dead wood for whatever you can get. It doesn't matter what it used to be worth; it's now worth what the market will bear. Try to return anything that isn't moving. You might even want to consider contacting a liquidator. Ultimately, the goal is to get the cash flowing so you will never run out of the main things.

PEOPLE

I have purposely saved the hardest cash-conserving technique for last. Some would have included it in the discussion of overhead or excess inventory. As a business owner, I know you see your people in the way I do: Your people are human beings. For many owners they become like family. To tell someone in your family that his or her services are no longer needed is gut-wrenching. However, your common sense needs to override your emotions when it relates to those who work with and for you.

Conventional wisdom holds that you look for ways to save everyone. I'm all for it if everyone is worth saving. Cutting back on hours, job-sharing, unpaid vacations, and changing some employees into independent contractors can help you reduce costs without letting people go. If, on the other hand, you have some underachievers, now is the time to take a cold, hard look at what they are costing your business.

It's equally important that you view individuals with current clarity. Not everyone in your organization can handle disruptive change. Don't allow your memory of past performance to cloud your current judgment. You're doing no one any favors by hanging onto underperforming employees. It's not helping you, it's not helping your customers, and perhaps most of all, it's not helping others in your organization who are performing at a higher level. While the pink-slipped employee may not agree with your decision today, you should know that the day will come when they will find a place to flourish.

This stuff isn't easy to do. It's not even easy to write about. Yet I do have one small piece of advice that might help to soften the blow for you and for your "family" of employees. As best you can, try not to allow anyone to be surprised by their termination. If you are giving your people timely feedback regarding their performance and the organization's financial health, they should see it coming.

Chapter 4

Keep Your Customers

The question is, then, do we try to make things easy on ourselves or do we try to make things easy on our customers, whoever they may be?

— Niccolo Machiavelli

■   ■   ■

Customer retention experts tell us that it costs five times more to get a new customer than to retain an existing one. I can remember first learning this handy fact as a young advertising executive. Chances are pretty good you've heard it too. It seems to make a lot of sense.

But unfortunately, this well-known truism isn't exactly true, at least not for you and me. It is just another myth that has been around for decades, reiterated over and over again in everything from MBA-level textbooks to trade association newsletters. If you put "five times," "new," and "customer" in Google, you will get over a million results, the majority of which refer to this "known fact." How did the notion get so well-entrenched in popular business-speak?

Apparently the fallacy is rooted in the research of the federal government's Technical Assistance Research Program (not to be confused with the recent TARP bank bailout, though the initials are the same). Much like McGraw-Hill report #5262, the older TARP produced a report with a very specific finding that has since been grossly overgeneralized. Former TARP president John Goodman has said on numerous occasions that findings attributed to TARP research range from "garbled and confused" to "outright wrong."

Working with a Big Three automaker in the 1970s and 1980s, one TARP study concentrated on the advertising cost to win new customers and compared it to "the goodwill expense" to retain current customers. How was something as nebulous as goodwill expense calculated? What were the specific forms of advertising used? Was the advertising-to-new-sale ratio a correlation or causation?

We'll never know, since the basic source data evidently no longer exists. What the report did say was that it cost $750 in advertising expense to get one new customer, versus $150 in goodwill expense—whatever that is—to retain an existing customer. The entire 5-to-1 ratio fallacy can be tracked back to this one finding. Later, author Frederick F. Reichheld found a similar ratio for established companies in his best-selling 1996 book, *The Loyalty Effect.*

If you were an automobile manufacturer or dealer doing business 30 years ago, or a financial services company in the mid-1990s, this ratio might have had some meaning. Subsequent TARP studies in other industries found "the real ratio of cost to win a customer versus retaining a current customer varies from 2 to 1 to 20 to 1," according to former president Goodman. In other words, if the 5-to-1 ratio applies to you, it is merely coincidental.

Here's my concern. Too many business owners abandon new customer acquisition activities because they believe the 5-to-1 ratio fallacy. They see it as too expensive. My question to you is a simple one. Are you so worried about how much you have to give up to get customers that you lose sight of how much they're going to potentially give you? For many businesses, it is possible to efficiently acquire and retain new customers, even in a downturn.

No matter what it costs you to acquire new customers, in a recession it is undoubtedly a good idea to first focus time, money, and effort on retaining your most important current customers. It is simple common sense. Eighty percent of your revenue is coming from 20 percent of your customers. This is a ratio that I know to be true. While the Pareto principle (the 80/20 rule) is often stretched into areas where it doesn't belong, I can personally attest to its validity with regard to sales revenue in hundreds of businesses that I've worked with over the years. Even if you are an exception to the rule, I urge you to calculate those customers that represent your best opportunity for generating right-away revenue. Because after all, cash is king; some of your best customers have it and you need it.

There are many ways to solidify your relationship with core customers in a downturn. Of course techniques vary by industry and customer. Here are a few questions

I suggest you answer regarding your critical sources of revenue.

ARE YOU OFFERING GREATER VALUE BEYOND JUST YOUR PRODUCT OR SERVICE?

We can assume that if customers are doing business with you currently, they already somewhat understand the value of the specific products and/or services they buy from you. One of your best ways to defend against inevitable price-cutting by competitors is to look for ways to add extra value to your offerings.

My dry cleaner is not the cheapest in the area, nor do I believe they're any better at cleaning and pressing. What has kept me loyal for more than 10 years is the cumulative effect of all the little things. At some point their system identified me as a valuable customer. As a result, I have a specially-tagged blue bag that I can drop off at a designated VIP drive-through window or a 24-hour drop box. They guarantee next-day service. They're open on Saturdays. When my order is ready to be picked up, they know my car and quickly run out with my rejuvenated shirts and suits.

Like any consumer these days, I've had to look at all my costs. While I have recently made significant changes after problems with my cable television and cell phone services, my dry cleaner's record is spotless.

ARE YOU MAKING IT EASY FOR YOUR BEST CUSTOMERS TO BE HEARD?

Big businesses rely on exasperating phone trees and interminable hold times before you can talk to a real person. Even when you do reach a living, breathing human being, they are often so far removed from actual decision makers that they can offer little in the way of real help. Unanswered e-mail questions are the norm, not the exception. You can do better than all this.

Your most valuable customers deserve exceptional response time to any type of inquiry, conflict, or new need. No matter how they choose to communicate with you, be sure they are only one quick step away from a decision maker or expert. Most businesses, big and small, do some kind of customer satisfaction survey. That's all well and good, but if you don't know what your top customers think about your business, you might want to consider setting this book aside and finding a way to open those channels of communication immediately.

HOW WELL DO YOU COMMUNICATE APPRECIATION?

Trite and hollow thank-yous don't work because we are bombarded with them. Bulk holiday greeting cards and e-mails don't cut it either. To be truly effective, your demonstration of appreciation needs to be unique, un-expected, and personal. Sometimes a call from the owner is all it takes to say, "We really value your business." One business I know well sends a special gift after landing any new contract—a particularly fluffy, king-sized pillow em-broidered with the words, "Rest assured . . . you're working with us now." This unique, unexpected, and personal ges-ture says more than mere words can convey.

How do you say thank you?

HAVE YOU CONSIDERED MY 40/20 RULE?

A few years ago, bored with the tired but true 80/20 rule, I uncovered a rule of my own. My 40/20 rule states that most businesses devote 40 percent of their resources—in terms of time, money, and effort—to the *bottom* 20 percent of their customers as measured by profit.

Despite this ratio being based on no scientific research whatsoever, I have discovered that most business own-ers readily agree with the premise. That is to say, most are willing to admit that they have a tendency to hang onto marginal customers. Sometimes these customers are overly needy, sucking time and energy out of the organi-zation. More often, your business and the customer are simply ill-suited for one another.

The idea that any customer is a good customer is conventional thinking, but it defies common sense. Logic should tell you that you are probably coddling customers who should be taking their business elsewhere. One of the best ways to focus on customers that really matter is to weed out those that really don't.

I'm not suggesting that all the customers in your bottom 20 percent should be automatically "gifted" back to your competitors. In businesses such as retail you can't stop people from walking in your doors just because they aren't profitable enough. Asking them to stay away would cause more harm than good. I am suggesting that if your business is the type that chooses whom to work with, you should be pruning customers who are simply not a good fit for your business, and your common sense tells you they never will be.

Chapter 5

Plan for Action

*The majority . . . meet with failure because of their lack
of persistence in creating new plans to take the place of
those which fail.*

          —Napoleon Hill, Think and Grow Rich

■ ■ ■

Too few business owners plan effectively. In my first book
I stated that effective planning was the best predictor
of whether or not a business would achieve sustainable
growth. In recent years, studies of privately held companies have consistently shown an irrefutable correlation.
Yet in my experience, fewer than 20 percent of business
owners see planning as a priority. Few argue that planning
isn't a good idea. They simply "don't have time."

If there's ever a period in which you need to make time
for planning, it's during a crisis. As Dwight D. Eisenhower
said, "Plans are useless, but planning is indispensable."
When you are trying to duck in order to recover, it's not
the plan itself that leads to success. It's the process of
effective planning that keeps you on the right path.

As an embattled business owner, growth may be the
furthest thing from your mind. However, there's no reason why growth shouldn't remain your ultimate goal.
When you find yourself in the midst of a storm created
by forces beyond your control, it may be necessary to

temporarily take your eyes off the long-term goal in order to successfully navigate the treacherous waters of economic uncertainty.

Imagine you are the captain of a commercial container ship, outfitted with the latest and greatest navigational aids and a crackerjack crew. Your goal is to get from Singapore to San Francisco, and you and your team have developed an appropriate navigational plan. The long-term goal is to safely and efficiently get your cargo from point A to point B.

Mother Nature has a plan of her own, however. A violent storm is brewing in the South Pacific, and prudence dictates that you seek safe harbor in the bay of a small island. Even at the height of the storm you don't abandon the ultimate goal; instead, you make the necessary detour to ensure your success.

In that small bay, no amount of previous planning or sophisticated navigational equipment is going to help you weather the storm. Indeed, a local islander's hand-drawn map of the bay's reefs is of more value to you than any GPS system or any chart of international shipping lanes. Depending on wind conditions, you might find yourself pointed in a direction opposite to your desired destination. That's okay. The most immediate need for your vessel and crew is for you to devise a prudent plan of survival.

If you are an embattled business owner, your present circumstance is much the same as that of the container ship captain. Everyone is depending on you to devise an immediate plan of action to avert present dangers.

No matter if you need to develop a long-term growth plan or an immediate mode of corrective action, the characteristics of a successful plan are the same. Let's call them *The 10 R's of Planning in a Crisis.*

1. Representative

No matter how good your plan is, it will always remain *your* plan. But to be truly effective, your course of action must represent the views of your entire team. If you have five employees, this should be relatively simple. If you have ten people in your customer service department alone, ask them to appoint a delegate who can bring their ideas and concerns to the table, and do the same for each of your departments. Good planning depends on a holistic approach to the organization's immediate challenges.

2. Research

The best source of relevant information is hidden somewhere in your organization. Competitive information might be in a salesperson's head. Important changes in your vendor relations might be buried on a purchasing manager's hard drive. As we've already seen, outside studies are often too general to be actionable. Most organizations have more data than they know what to do with. Find a way to turn data into information from which you can glean insights. If your trade association has done a recent report that is directly related to you, then by all means include that in your planning process.

3. Remote

In order to plan effectively, it is best to get away from the distraction of the day-to-day. Find an appropriate off-site meeting space that offers a high level of privacy at a low price. For the cost of lunch for a few people, restaurants will often throw in the use of a private room for free. The purpose is to gain quiet clarity for everyone involved. In no way should these events be misconstrued as anything but roll-up-the-sleeves work sessions. "Retreat" also starts with an R, but I'm not using that word for a reason.

4. Realistic

I don't know whether you play golf. I don't. But I know that environmental conditions can affect the world's greatest players. Even if you are still shooting par, plan for some bogies during the next few quarters. How will the current economic storm potentially affect organizational performance? In a recession, a truly realistic plan anticipates the potential for destructive domino effects.

5. Results-Oriented

In order to build an effective plan, it is imperative that it include specific results. To decrease workmen's compensation claims by 20 percent is specific. To increase monthly time spent on safety training from

50 man-hours to 75 in the next two months is very specific. The first is a goal; the second is an action step to achieve the expressed goal. Being specific about little things makes big things happen.

6. Responsibilities

There's no way to put a plan into action unless someone owns it. Who is responsible for what and when? Regardless of their job descriptions, allow your people to champion the things they care about most. If someone on your marketing staff feels compelled to research a more efficient purchasing system, I say let her. Crisis planning calls for people to try on a few different hats.

7. (w)Ritten

Things we think we could never forget are often lost if they are not written down immediately. By writing down the relevant actions, ideas, responsibilities, and timetables, the plan becomes of much greater value. For one thing, it can be more easily shared throughout the organization. Somehow, the mere act of writing something down also gives it more importance. Remember, this plan is an ongoing process, not an event. Re-dos and revisions should not only be expected, but encouraged.

8. Repeated

There's a tendency to lose momentum after the initial plan is created. Don't let this happen. Regularly repeating the plan in all forms of communication is an important part of the planning process. It's incumbent upon you to get the word out fast and frequently. By doing so, you dampen the din of the gossip mill and keep everyone on the same page—literally.

9. Real-Time Monitoring

I believe we've reached a point where anyone in your organization should be able to push a few buttons and get an accurate view of where they stand versus the plan. Why not? Our technology can do it. At the very least, you should have an easy-to-read daily one-page report posted for all to see. How did we do yesterday versus the plan? How are things looking for the month? Planning requires vigilant oversight by everyone. If you want them to be involved, real-time feedback is a great way to engage them.

10. Regularly Updated

As circumstances dictate, your plan for averting present dangers will require revision. There's no right interpretation of the meaning of the word "regularly." If you are a mortgage broker it might be weekly. If you are a ball-bearing producer, quarterly reviews might serve your needs. As a business owner, defining how and when to review your course of action is one of the most important roles you take on as a leader.

Chapter 6

TRUST and Your People

I meet literally thousands of business owners every year, and I see a wide variety of types—full-throttle entrepreneurs who create a sizable wake in their path; the unassuming mom-and-pops content to putter along year after year; the talented craftspeople who builds their business one brick at a time; the former corporate castoff who becomes a business owner by necessity rather than choice.

Regardless of how you came to be a business owner, it's important to recognize that, up to this point, you have developed a style that works for you. This may be the time to reassess it.

In this era of unprecedented uncertainty, the people who work with and for you are understandably frightened. Their fear may have nothing to do with you. No one has emerged unscathed from this tumultuous economy, and it's fear of the unknowable future that's really got everybody spooked. As a result, your people are looking for something—or someone—they can trust. They are not looking to follow an entrepreneur, an artisan, or a manager. They are looking to follow a leader. They are looking to follow you.

Your style may be wholly appropriate in the present environment, or it may not. Regardless of how you've managed before, I suggest that the best way to get your people to follow you is to *earn their TRUST*.

Timely

Realistic

Unscripted

Sensitive

Transparent

TIMELY

Thomas Edison once said, "Time is really the only capital that any human being has. . . ." At a time like this, time is of the essence. If the ticking clock didn't matter, you'd be apt to make better decisions and the people that work around you would notice. Unfortunately, in a crisis time becomes compressed. When you are embattled, prompt actions and decisions become paramount. As we have already learned about business triage, prioritization is a leader's job. That makes it your job.

Your team is relying on you to identify and address the organization's most pressing issues in a timely manner. Don't revert back to your default setting—whatever you know best. Figure out what really needs to be done and get it done quickly and effectively. This isn't about putting in more hours. It's about putting more in the hours that are available to you. Knee-jerk reaction is not what I am calling for. Instead, I am urging you to prioritize the areas that need immediate attention, communicate those priorities to the people who can affect them, and take the best possible course of action.

As a leader, the only thing you can hope to do is make the best decision at a crucial moment. The one thing you can't allow yourself to do is put off decisions that demand action. Employees will support informed decisiveness, even if it proves to be a less than perfect path. Indecision fosters fear.

REALISTIC

As the word applies to planning, "realistic" refers to what can be reasonably achieved. It also means getting your people to face challenges head on. One of the greatest threats to your business today is your employees' inability to accept the new reality. Business as usual is over for now, yet your employees will have a difficult time dealing with fundamental change.

Successful business leaders encourage their people to find a new sense of purpose in a changing environment. Pie-in-the-sky optimism is not realistic. Conversely, overcompensating with crash-and-burn fatalism does your team little good. Your people deserve a realistic assessment of where the business is at the moment—all the bad and all the good—and how it affects them. When you are able to accurately convey the new reality, they are in turn able to find more resourceful ways in which to contribute. Be sure to listen to their ideas for constructive problem solving.

Don't allow fear to fester in the ranks. Everyone already knows these are tough times. Regardless of how daunting the challenges you face, your people can rise to the occasion better if they truly understand them. Now is the time to get real.

UNSCRIPTED

Once you have prioritized your challenges in a timely manner and are prepared to deliver a realistic assessment to the troops, recognize that how you deliver that information becomes as important as the information itself. These days everyone is a skeptic, and why shouldn't they be? We live in a world where much of the information that comes to us is rightly viewed as self-serving, partisan, and tainted by distorted half-truths. Peoples' cynicism has a reached a point where even the truth can become suspect if not conveyed properly.

What your people need is authenticity. Find ways to speak plainly and from the heart. Don't send a memo. A bullet-driven PowerPoint presentation is not going to do the trick. They need to hear the news directly from you. Try to avoid the clichéd, hackneyed, and rote speech. Decide what needs to be said, say it in a way that everyone can understand, and make sure it prompts an open dialogue. Know what you need to say so well that you don't need a script.

SENSITIVE

I'm not suggesting you pull everyone together so they can hold hands and sing "Kum Ba Yah." Instead I am using the word sensitive as synonymous with perceptive. As best you can, hone your observation skills. Become acutely aware of even small changes in your organization's attitude and behaviors. Look for the broader meaning of the little things you hear and see.

In the past, closely monitoring your people's performance may have been all that really mattered. Now, you must look for nuanced signs in what your people say and do. No matter how distracted you are by current circumstances, it is in your best interest to turn up the sensitivity on your people meter.

For some, this is a natural way of leading. For others, the ability to read complex social situations is difficult. No matter how you are built, find ways to improve your ability to gain insights from your people's subtle signals. If you want to lead people in new directions, you must better understand what they are thinking but not explicitly saying.

TRANSPARENT

An eastern adage says, "Only three things cannot be hidden: the sun, the moon, and the truth." Some business owners keep their employees in the dark about everything.

Others embrace a totally open-book style of management. Chances are you fall somewhere in the middle, and I'm not suggesting that you necessarily change. However, I am recommending that you reevaluate how transparent you are in regard to your business.

"Transparency" is a word being thrown around a lot these days. How it's used in high finance and governance has little relevance to a business owner. For you, transparent leadership requires you to be forthcoming with information that your people need in order to be effective. They don't need to know how much salary you are pulling out of the business. They don't need to know how you choose to allocate business and personal expenses. However, they have every right to know when a key account is in jeopardy of being lost. They need to be told when a supplier has chosen to cut you off. Trying to insulate your employees from bad news is a bad idea. They're going to find out anyway, and uninformed chatter often makes the problem sound worse than it really is.

A transparent business leader knows that when people perceive they are fully informed, they are more likely to become committed to the leader's business.

■ ■ ■

TRUST is about tapping into the power of individuals. As a business owner, understand that people are more attuned to "being spun" than ever before. The only logical response is for you to truly earn their TRUST.

Chapter 7

Enlist Outside Expertise

Mental illness is something nobody likes to talk about. In fact, I'm willing to wager that just reading that sentence made you a little uncomfortable.

Due to its prevalence, clinical depression is often called the common cold of mental illness. While statistics vary due to definitions and diagnoses, the National Institute of Mental Health estimates that about five percent of people in the United States will suffer some form of clinical depression in their adult life. If you have ever known someone who suffered with it, then you know it's not a character flaw or something they could simply snap out of.

Today we know a lot more about depression than ever before. Experts estimate that over 80 percent of people who seek treatment are significantly helped within a couple of weeks. Unfortunately, the stigma surrounding clinical depression results in only one-third of those afflicted seeking help. Effective help is readily available, but those suffering have to ask for it.

Embattled business owners behave in much the same way. No matter how overwhelming their condition, most choose to stoically soldier on alone. If you are feeling overwhelmed, admit it to yourself. You're not the first, nor will you be the last business owner to become immobilized by circumstances that seem to be beyond your control. I say "seem to be" because in most cases there is a way out. Sometimes your head is just spinning so fast you can't see it.

Raising your hand and asking for help is not a weakness. It's a strength. It takes a strong person to admit he doesn't know what to do next, especially if he has experienced years of smooth sailing.

Conventional wisdom suggests that you enlist outside expertise. Too many owners take this to mean they should seek advice from those closest to them and their business. However, common sense should tell you that those closest are often too close to be objective.

A trusted family member or friend can offer a few good points but may be reluctant to focus your attention on anything that makes either of you uncomfortable. People you are currently paying for advice also have difficulty with objectivity. Even if it's unconscious, they have a vested interest in telling you what you want to hear. Consider your accountant, for example.

In a 2002 Harvard Business School experiment, researchers divided more than 100 accountants into two equal groups. The groups were separated and given the same ambiguous auditing information. In other words, the information was purposely left open to interpretation. The first group was asked to assume they were being paid by the audited company. The second group was told they had been retained by a different company doing business with the audited organization. So the second group believed they were not being directly paid by the audited company.

The results were telling. Accountants from the first group were 30 percent more likely to conclude that the audited data met Generally Accepted Accounting Principles (GAAP). The second group was much less likely to side with the audited company. Even in this controlled experiment, where no actual relationships existed, the group told to assume they were being paid directly was significantly more likely to agree with their client's judgment. Imagine the overt influence you, the persuasive, charismatic business owner, can have over any paid advisor in the real world.

When you are suffering and seeking help, the most important attribute of an advisor is objectivity. Objective help is available to you from a wide variety of outside resources. If money is particularly tight, you may want to consider seeking help from groups such as local Small Business Development Centers (SBDCs); local institutes of higher learning; SCORE (Service Corps of Retired Executives); or the Small Business Administration (SBA). Groups like these defy conventional wisdom in that you often get back far more than what you pay to work with them.

I'm also a big believer in Chambers of Commerce. Many offer great learning opportunities at a very low cost. Every industry also has local, regional, and national associations whose sole mission is to help you further your cause. Tap into their collective wisdom.

Of course, there are professional consultants offering everything from inventory management expertise to complete turnaround solutions. While such a consultant may cost more, economies of scale may make one of these experts your best option. I always tell my prospective consulting clients that they are smart enough to figure most things out on their own, given enough time, but time is money. If I can't save them both, and thereby more than pay for myself, I shouldn't be hired in the first place. I believe most consultants working with business owners would agree with that approach, but I certainly can't speak for all of them. No matter what the cost, checking multiple references on any advisor is well worth your time before you spend any money.

I've saved my most important advisor advice for last. Any privately held business can be well-served by an informal advisory board. By informal I mean there is no legal entanglement for you or for them. By advisory board, I am referring to a regular gathering of knowledgeable individuals whose only interest is to see your company succeed. Their job is to tell you the truth and hold your feet to the fire. While their advice is never binding, it always helps to have an impartial group to whom you have to answer. They might say to you: "I thought you said you were going to get out of that market," or "Didn't you tell us three months ago that this situation would be fixed by now?" or "Sounds like you are still having problems with your insurance. I know just the right person who can help."

Once again, the key here is the objectivity of an outsider. I suggest you look for three to five local business leaders who bring unique strengths to the table. Most small business owners assume that the people they would most like to recruit are too busy or wouldn't be interested. My experience has been exactly the opposite. Most are honored to be asked and find the experience enriching.

Here are some other important considerations when putting together your advisory board:

- The advisors should have no financial interest in your business. No customers, vendors, paid professionals, or family members.
- Look for expertise that fills your knowledge gaps.
- Most leaders will serve on your board for free. However, I have found that at least a token honorarium says you value their time.
- How often to meet should be the first agenda item at the first meeting. Let your advisors gauge the need for frequency.
- If someone is not contributing or misses a couple of meetings, move quickly to make a change.
- Be sure that you are always fully prepared for each gathering. Send a detailed agenda prior to the meeting and stick to it. Normally, you can get what you need done in less than two hours if you are organized.

Chapter 8

Maintain Your Marketing

Ask yourself how many shots you would have saved if you ... always developed a strategy before you hit, and always played within your own capabilities.

—Jack Nicklaus

■ ■ ■

As we've learned, it's not difficult to find reports, studies, and expert opinions about the need to maintain your marketing during a recession. I fear that too many leaders miss the true meaning of this prevailing wisdom.

For example, most business owners use the terms "marketing" and "advertising" interchangeably. Or, more specifically, they say marketing when they actually mean advertising. If you're the exception to the rule, please don't take exception. Indeed, if you're among the minority that does understand the difference, chances are you already know that what I am saying is true.

This distinction isn't just one of semantics. When revenues are falling, too many business owners jump on specific advertising tactics before they've reconsidered their broader marketing strategies. What is marketing? Peter Drucker, otherwise known as the father of modern management, once quipped, "Marketing is everything." For me, marketing includes all the ways you look to differentiate your product or service in the marketplace.

I am also troubled by the possible misunderstanding of the word "maintain." Maintain can be defined as "keeping things as they are." If you read the meaning the way I do, you understand the need to emphasize the ongoing investment of time, money, and effort to meet the ever-changing needs of the marketplace. If, on the other hand, you regard maintaining as an excuse to keep doing what you've always done, then count me out (especially if it isn't working).

To sum up: "Maintain Your Marketing" does not mean "keep spending on the same advertising vehicles you've always used, regardless of how effective they are." It does mean you should look for ways to differentiate your offerings so you can more efficiently retain and even acquire attractive customers. Look to maintain your marketing emphasis in these specific areas.

BRANDING STRATEGIES

Staying true to your brand identity is critical in the present time of crisis. What is your brand identity? Whether you've actively designed a branding strategy or not, you do have a brand identity, which is the perception of your business's specific position in the collective mind of the marketplace. Your brand is the sum total of all the ways in which you present yourself. When presented properly, your brand identity clearly differentiates you from competitors. In fact, branding can put your business in a position where it has no direct competition.

Early in my career, I helped develop advertising for some great consumer and business-to-business brands. In three small, fast-growth companies where I served as president, "branding" was certainly one of the secrets to our success. I'm a big believer in the power of branding, even for micro-businesses that don't think branding applies to them. However, and let me be as clear as possible about this, a time of crisis is not the time to make a wholesale change to your brand identity. Instead, you've got to be who you are, but even more so.

When you've spent years establishing a luxury positioning, it doesn't make sense to get down in the mud with the low-cost leaders. If you've built your reputation as a service leader, now may be the time to take your service levels one step further, not one step back. As you consider your various marketing strategy options, never forget that any incremental changes are more likely to prove successful if they dovetail with your existing brand identity. Also remember that the marketplace is telling you where you should consider change. This isn't the time for personal druthers and gut hunches.

INNOVATION STRATEGIES

For any business, innovation is an essential way to differentiate. Whether it's an effort to create new products and services that stand apart, a pricing model that adds perceived value in an exciting new way, or a game-changing distribution strategy, the need to innovate is more important now than ever before. Innovative thinking and implementation don't have to cost a lot of money. This recession will undoubtedly create big opportunities that might call for some bigger risks later. When ducking, however, look for innovative ways to meet the market that don't require an enormous cash investment.

When I was president of a hard hat manufacturer in the early 1990s, our sales were falling along with the drop in commercial and residential construction. As patriotism began to run high during the first Persian Gulf War, requests for hard hats imprinted with American flags on the side began to trickle in. Within months, this low-cost "innovation" to our existing product became our best-selling and most profitable item. The hard hat market pie may have been shrinking, but we were getting a bigger slice of it simply by responding to the changing market.

To innovate while in the duck position, listen to the marketplace and look for quick and relatively inexpensive ways to meet its needs. Organizations focused on survival often lose their innovative spirit. Create an environment where new ways of looking at old offerings are rewarded.

DISTRIBUTION STRATEGIES

Most business owners believe that their choice in distribution channels is unrelated to marketing. Actually, how you choose to go to market is one of the most important aspects of marketing.

In a recession, the chances that your existing supply chains will be disrupted increase dramatically. My guess is they already have been disrupted for you to some extent, but you must assume the worst is yet to come. I'm not predicting that the worst will actually happen, but I am telling you to assume that the unexpected could occur.

Getting clearer on your potential options in channel partners is vital to your business. We live in a time when any partner you depend on now may not be around when you need them. No matter how financially strong your current suppliers, vendors, distributors, or agents may appear today, contingency planning will put you in a better position. Taking the time to thoroughly vet both existing and potential partners now will put you in a better position to avoid a possible catastrophe.

Later, we will consider the possible growth opportunities in your distribution strategies. When ducking, the proper position is to keep your distribution options open.

SALES STRATEGIES

I recently spoke at a sales conference for a large multinational corporation. The new leadership team had brought their entire worldwide sales force of 5,000 to a three-day learning event. The sole purpose of the meeting was to convey the substantial changes being made to their marketing plan. Everything from their products to their target markets to their unique selling proposition had been revamped to meet the needs of a changing marketplace.

As I listened to the leaders speak all morning, they made a lot of sense to me. I spoke just before lunch and told the assembled sales associates that I agreed with the leadership's new direction. However, I later learned at lunch that many of the tenured pros were less than enthusiastic about what they had heard from their new leaders. It wasn't that they believed it or didn't believe it; they were simply jaded. This was their third "reorg" in the last seven years. In their mind, they had heard this all before and sales had remained flat through it all.

I feel sorry for big organizations. For them, communicating even a can't-miss new plan can take months to actually sink in—if it ever does.

That's not true for you. In a privately held business, those responsible for selling your products and services are relatively few in number. By working directly with them, getting buy-in to a new marketing plan should be much easier. True sales professionals aren't the easiest cats to herd, but it's a heck of a lot easier when you don't have thousands of them to corral. Be sure that any and all changes to your marketing initiatives include input from those closest to your current customers: outside sales representatives, inside sales support staff, independent reps, and so on.

One of the most common mistakes business owners make with their sales efforts is not segmenting properly. Too often segmentations are based on arbitrary criteria such as geography or size of customer. (Do you have A, B, and C accounts?) The best way to segment, especially in a downturn, is by individual expertise and customer type.

I once worked closely with a distributor of "blank" promotional apparel. In the downturn following 9/11, their sales began to crumble. They changed their sales segmentation from one of north/south/east/west to one of screen printers, embroiderers, ad specialties, and the uniform market. By segmenting their customers by type, and their salespeople by expertise, they were better able to serve each group's specific needs. The quick response served to solidify their most important relationships.

MARKETING COMMUNICATIONS (MARCOM) STRATEGIES

Marketing communications is the broad term used to describe all the ways in which you can trumpet your differentiation to your targeted markets. It includes everything from traditional advertising and public relations to promotional e-mails and web sites. While the vehicles vary, the purpose is the same: to remind existing customers and inform potential customers of the relevant ways in which your business offers them unique value.

Marcom is a science and an art. How you choose to employ it is crucial to the lasting success of your business. Yet, I recommend that you proceed with caution.

Marketing communications wouldn't exist if it didn't work. That is a given. The question is how much should you spend on Marcom when times are tight? Now is not the time to spend money on maybes. Maybe we should try those in-home coupons like we did the last time things got slow? Maybe we could exhibit in a new trade show this year? Maybe if we keep running those same radio spots, something good will finally happen.

Before you spend another Marcom dollar, honestly answer these five questions:

1. Do we have a history of successful marketing communication efforts?

2. Do we have a strong understanding of how creative communications enhance our differentiation?

3. Do we know how to measure the results of all our Marcom spending?

4. Are we able to track the lifetime value of customers we both gain and retain with our various Marcom investments?

5. Is our Marcom mix like a warm shower? Have we learned how to adjust a couple of knobs to get the precise temperature we need, when we need it?

When ducking, there should be little doubt in your mind that your Marcom investments have a quantifiable payback in a predictable amount of time. If you don't know how to effectively communicate your message in a cost-efficient manner, now is not the time to experiment with your all important cash. If you are spending on a specific program now, and you don't know if it's really working, then turn it off. If you do know what you're doing, and it's obviously working, then turn up the pressure on your competition!

I know one business owner in home maintenance services who recently "shut off" her entire multi-market yellow pages budget of $150,000 per year and put it all back into what she knew was working for her: cost-per-click banner advertising on local websites. Her bold move was born of measurable data that she turned into actionable information.

After she told me her story at a local conference, she asked me what I thought about her decision. I first congratulated her for knowing what was working and having the courage to go "all in." I told her it was clearly a good move for her company.

However, I couldn't help but caution her that if I were her competitor, the first thing I would do is to attack her where she has chosen not to defend. I'd increase my yellow pages exposure and offer a substantial incentive to "mention this ad and receive . . ." Then I would track the heck out of it to be sure it was paying us back.

When it comes to the art and science of marketing communications in a downturn, it often makes sense to zig while everyone else is zagging.

Chapter 9

Price for Profit

Of all the marketing issues to be considered during the duck phase, pricing is probably the most challenging of all. Conventional thinking tells you to maintain your prices as long as you can. Yet, the "cut prices" reflex is a strong one, and if you're desperate for cash, it may be an inevitable, albeit unattractive, tourniquet to be applied.

But let's consider pricing within the context of the duck posture. If you're trying to put yourself in the best position to counterpunch later, slashing prices today can dilute your perceived value in the market for years to come. By cutting your profit margins, you may be setting your organization up for even greater financial hardship in the near future. Of course, without sales volume, you may not have a future at all.

So what is the right answer on pricing while ducking in a recession? There actually isn't one, but I do know a few of the right questions you need to ask yourself.

ARE YOU OVER-RELIANT ON PRICING FORMULAS?

Every industry has conventional wisdom about how to price. For instance, I once worked closely with a regional shoe retailer. "A keystone and two and that will do" was the owner's only pricing strategy. In other words, he'd simply double the price he paid for a pair of shoes and tack on two dollars. If they didn't sell, he would mark them down 50 percent. Contractors the world over use a cost-plus model. Manufacturers try to hit a specific gross margin. This makes pricing easy, but rarely is it the best strategy.

Relying on formulaic thinking defies common sense. No one pricing formula makes sense for the breadth and depth of a business's products and services. Pricing based on perceived value is the way you should look at it. High-volume, quick-turning items might be priced aggressively. Maybe. Customization should command a premium. Maybe. The point is pricing based on a formula is never a good idea for your business, especially in a volatile market. In the end, it's the pricing mix that matters.

By the way, "standard payment terms" is one of my least favorite pricing formulas. Many view their terms as a financial consideration and not a pricing (and therefore marketing) strategy. Years ago, offering every customer the same terms might have made some sense in order to achieve greater administrative efficiency. Today, information technology allows us to customize payment terms to meet an individual customer's needs.

If your terms are net 30, how much of a discount are you willing to offer for up-front payments? How much more do you need to charge to make 90-day terms more attractive for you? While cash is certainly king, meeting a customer need may be queen. Find a way to make your terms a true differentiator. If you don't, somebody else will.

ARE YOU CHARGING A PRICE FOR
EVERYTHING YOU SHOULD BE?

I once worked with the owner of an industrial products distributorship. The company imported lines of high-tech equipment from Asia and Europe for the food processing industry. Every product installed was invoiced once. The price included not only the machine but also the installation, training, and ongoing phone support for every customer.

After we studied the situation together, the owner realized his "one price fits all" strategy wasn't working for anyone. Larger customers fully staffed with experienced engineers didn't need any training or phone support. Smaller operations and start-ups, on the other hand, needed constant hand-holding. By separating the price of a shipped machine from the installation, training, and support, the importer became not only more competitive but more profitable.

Are you leaving money on the table? Even in a recession, your customers may be willing to pay for something of value that you've been giving away. An airline charging for checked baggage after decades of giving the service away is in a desperate attempt to stay alive. That is not what I am recommending. Instead, I urge you to look at your products and see if there is a value-added service the market will embrace. Similarly, if you are a service organization, a good/better/best product model might make sense. Does charging a flat hourly rate for your services meet the needs of every potential customer?

Your customers understand value. Do you?

ARE YOU NEGOTIATING PRICE AT THE RIGHT LEVEL?

In many businesses there are multiple people involved in a purchasing decision. The astute owner understands that price and value are often perceived differently by different people.

I know the owner of a specialty bakery. She figured out that no matter how many times a young bride-to-be and her friends came to discuss wedding cake options, the bride's mother was the ultimate decision maker. The friends were influencers, the bride was a specifier, but mom was the check writer. The more the baker could connect with the mother, the more likely she was to seal the deal.

The friends cared about the cake decorating. The bride added taste to the equation. For the mother, re-liability and reputation mattered most. Mom's broader perspective makes her less price sensitive than the friend or would-be bride if left to their own devices. For the mother, assurance that the cake will arrive at the reception hall safely and on time is a very important determinant.

Her ability to brag to friends and family about getting it at the best shop in town is the most important criterion. (Dad, left sitting in the car, is usually the silent partner in this transaction.)

The same dynamics hold true in any business-to-business relationship. The guy in shipping asking for a new computerized scale that fully integrates with all his shipping vendors is a "specs" influencer. The purchasing agent is looking to squeeze out the best possible price while getting the requisition request off her desk as soon as possible. The owner of the business is most likely concerned with overall value. Price often takes a back seat to warranties, reputation for reliability, and the system's overall "scalability."

In my experience, dealing with the individual who can factor in the broader context of your overall value proposition is a winning pricing strategy. The higher the level at which you negotiate, the lower the tendency to focus on price alone.

DO YOU MENTALLY SEPARATE PROFIT *MARGIN* FROM SALES *VOLUME*?

Most business owners say they consider both margin and volume equally when they set pricing, but too often their behavior suggests otherwise. Try this purposely simplified accounting experiment, and see how you do. Whatever you do, please don't over-think it; there is no trick here.

Let's say you own a business that manufactures duck decoys. Each decoy costs $6 in raw material and $4 in labor to produce. You sell the ducks for $15 a unit. Your business will spend $250,000 in General and Administrative (G&A) expenses and $200,000 in Sales and Marketing (S&M) during the year. You have contracts for 100,000 units to be delivered over the next 12 months, meaning your sales will be $1.5 million. While unit sales will be down significantly from last year, your accountant projects that this scenario should still net you an operating profit of $50,000 on the year. Here's how:

Sales	$1,500,000	100 %
Materials	600,000	40.0%
Labor	400,000	26.7%
Cost of Sales	$1,000,000	66.7%
Gross Profit	500,000	33.3%
G&A	250,000	16.7%
S&M	200,000	13.3%
Operating Profit	$ 50,000	3.3%

You calculate that your total cost per unit will be $14.50 (because your labor and material costs are $10 per unit and your G&A and S&M costs total $4.50 per unit at 100,000 units sold.) Your gross profit margin will be

33.3 percent and your net operating profit before taxes will be 3.3 percent. Not too bad in a recession, embattled business owner. It's certainly better than a loss.

You've just finished reviewing your projected calculation for the year, when the phone rings. It's the federal government, and they need lots of duck decoys and they need them now. In fact, they require a total of 50,000 decoys to be delivered over the course of the next 12 months. One catch: They are budgeted to spend only $11.01 per duck. They will pay you up front for each delivery, and your plant has the capacity to produce the additional decoys.

Do you take the order?

You do if you want to more than double your profit for the year.

You can take time to do the math or you can just trust me on this one. Adding the 50,000 units at $11.01 a unit to the mix improves your bottom line profit from $50,000 to $100,500. How? Here is the simplest way to look at this: You will make more money selling 150,000 ducks at an average selling price of $13.67 than you will selling 100,000 ducks at $15.

Any cost accounting expert will tell you that this is a very simplistic model. I have purposely left out complicating issues ranging from energy costs to shipping expenses to the potential lost opportunity for higher margin orders that could come your way later in the year. Yet the core concept here is an important one: You should always weigh the proper balance of margin and volume when looking for the best possible pricing mix for your business.

There is an old saying that is both conventional wisdom and common sense: "Revenue is vanity, margin is sanity, but cash is king." I'm not an accountant, but I know that too many business owners keep score with conventional percentages, forgetting that the bottom line is the way to win. For instance, by taking this duck decoy order your gross margin percentage will be significantly reduced, making it appear unattractive at first glance. However, in the game called business, the best way to keep score is with money, not margins. It makes no difference if you own a manufacturing concern, a service company, or a retail store. Margins matter, but more often than not, the cash created by a better bottom-line matters more.

With these principles in mind, you should be ready to ride out any storm. Things are going to be bumpy, but that's hardly a secret. If you keep your head down but your mind open, the duck phase will properly position your organization for the smoother recovery phase ahead.

In order to duck effectively, be sure you develop:

- A sound cash management monitoring system, encompassing *all* of the relevant data.

- A realistic understanding of which customers are worth the effort to retain.

- An organizational environment that fosters TRUST in the people who work with and for you.

- A diligent effort to create a crisis plan that is written, communicated, and regularly updated.
- A well-rounded team of objective, expert advisors.
- A comprehensive marketing strategy that puts you in the best position to seize the inevitable opportunities created by change.

Section II

Growth Opportunities

On April 12, 1959, John F. Kennedy, on the campaign trail in his run for the presidency, told a gathering in Indianapolis, Indiana: "When written in Chinese, the word 'crisis' is composed of two characters. One represents danger and the other represents opportunity." In the decades since, respected news outlets from Reuters to the *Wall Street Journal* and political leaders like Richard Nixon, Condoleezza Rice, and Al Gore have also invoked this valuable lesson.

The only problem is it's not true. One Chinese character does convey the notion of "danger." The other really means "a crucial point in time." Victor H. Mair, a professor of Chinese language and literature at the University of Pennsylvania, says the longevity of this misperception, the continued quoting of the idea, is due to "wishful thinking." We want it to be true, so we readily accept it as fact.

You don't have to have a PhD in common sense to know that danger is dangerous. No rational business owner actively seeks a situation fraught with unnecessary risk. The prudent business leader understands that it is in fact change, not danger, from which opportunity emerges. By focusing on immediacy, or ducking, you have now put yourself in a stronger position to both recognize and seize opportunity. We don't need Chinese characters to tell us that. It just makes sense.

"Duck" is the ability to put your business in a ready position. Once you've gotten your ducks in a row, it's time to look for the opportunities afforded by change.

Chapter 10

Get Out of Your Bunker

Nothing in life is to be feared, it is only to be understood. Now is the time to understand more, so that we may fear less.

—Marie Curie

■   ■   ■

When you are truly embattled, survival is the first order of business. But once you've withstood the barrage of attacks, it's time to poke your head up and look around. If you don't see any immediate dangers and all you hear is the distant rumble of trouble, it's time to mobilize yourself and your troops. It's time to get out of your bunker.

I sit on a lot of airplanes. Over the last few months I couldn't help but notice a dramatic new trend. Airlines have been discounting heavily in an effort to fill their seats. Consumers have reacted to the bargains, and most flights I'm on these days are filled with young families and their children going to visit relatives, retired couples looking for a cheap getaway, or fresh-faced kids on their way to boot camp. What I'm not seeing are the laptop-toting business travelers.

I recently went through security at Dallas-Ft. Worth Airport at 5:00 P.M. on a Thursday. I had anticipated a long security line, but I got through in less than half the time it would normally take. I casually asked the TSA agent standing on the other side of the metal detector, "Where is everybody?"

"Families prefer to travel in the morning, sir, and business people aren't traveling at all right now," he answered. It turns out that he was the supervisor of this particular security checkpoint and had been for three years. He told me that the normal flow had been 4,000 people on a given weekday afternoon shift. He said it was now averaging about 1,300.

Once I reached the gate I got a free upgrade to first class. I boarded the plane and was seated next to a fellow road warrior who sold expensive telecom tools. I recounted the story the TSA agent had just told me and she had more to add. "This is my last trip for a while," she said. "My company just cut all travel until further notice—no exceptions."

Can you see your opportunity here?

When the economy falters, big and small companies alike make arbitrary edicts that defy common sense. Conventional wisdom is to cut discretionary spending, but it defies logic to apply such a crude tourniquet. The telecom equipment sales rep was off to visit a $500,000 account. I can't imagine how her company couldn't justify the $500 to send her on this trip again in the months ahead. Clearly, spending $500 to visit an important account is not discretionary. It's a must-do, especially if competitors aren't showing up.

It's not just air travel. Too many insurance agents, attorneys, and financial planners wait in their offices for the phone to ring or for customers to walk through the door. If embattled, now is your time to go to the customers. If your retail foot traffic is down, this may be the time to create an out-of-store event that increases your community exposure. The point is, while others continue their "we're under siege" bunker behavior, you have an opportunity to solidify relationships like never before.

Extricating yourself from the day-to-day battles should now be your marching orders. Spending more time in the office, plant, or shop won't put you on the path to long-term growth. Getting out and about and looking for possibilities is a key to your future success.

Here are some ways in which you can more clearly see the future of your opportunity.

GET FACE-TO-FACE WITH VENDORS AND CUSTOMERS

I'll take it one step further and say it may even make sense to visit your vendors' vendors and your customers' customers. You can never know too much about your business's supply chain, and it is unquestionably changing right now. Go see people of influence. I've never visited a channel partner and failed to learn something important. You'll never know what you're missing if you're not there, face-to-face.

Encouraging existing partners and potential partners to visit you and your team is important too. See more salespeople than ever before. Ask them how you can make more money together. Invite other leaders to your place of business and ask for their input.

Phone calls, e-mails, and video conferences all have their place, yet nothing can take the place of face-to-face relationships. Whether it takes a short drive across town or a long flight across the hemisphere, the value of seeing and hearing what others are doing and saying cannot be overestimated. Be sure your eyes and ears are open wide enough to perceive all the possibilities that represent future opportunities.

I recently visited the leaders of an association that had hired me to speak at their annual convention. They had not asked me to come before the meeting, but I was in town and found time to stop by. My purpose was to get detailed information for my upcoming keynote address. An hour later, we had reached an agreement for me to help their newly elected president improve his public speaking skills. Just showing up made the difference. You'll never know what you're missing if you're not there.

GET INVOLVED IN YOUR COMMUNITY

By community, I mean everything from your Chamber of Commerce to your national association. At the local level, I'm a big believer in the power of associated effort. There are thousands of Chambers in this country. Many can help you. Some may need your help. Either way, it is in your best interest that your local chamber, economic development corporation, and educational institutions really know you and your business.

Too often, business owners tell me they don't have enough time to get involved in organizations like these. They are apt to say, "There's nothing in it for me." The business owners I know that have sustained, profitable growth over a long period of time are invariably active in their local organizations. I don't know which is the cart and which is the horse on this one; I only know that visibility and growth appear to go together.

The same holds true at the national and even international level. Industry associations, annual conferences, and technical symposiums afford you the opportunity not only to increase your visibility but also to learn from your peers. Getting involved in your national association can mean sitting on the committee charged with lobbying efforts at the state and federal level. Active involvement in the legislation and regulations that directly affect you makes sense. It's also a tremendous opportunity to forge potential partnerships that would not have happened otherwise.

Today the term community has taken on even broader meaning. Social networking tools such as Facebook, MySpace, Twitter, and LinkedIn are quickly moving from teenage gossip to industry insights. Associations and trade publications host message boards that many business owners find invaluable. While a path to direct monetization may be less than clear, virtual communities represent potential goldmines for getting and giving valuable information.

MAKE THE MOST OF TRADE SHOWS

When managed properly, trade shows represent tremendous opportunities. In your duck phase, you may have been forced to scale back or cut your participation. However, now is the time to get back in the game. Trade shows should be much more than just a booth and a brochure. They are an opportunity to efficiently meet existing customers, potential customers, and all types of partners.

With trade shows, it's not enough just to show up. Pre- and post-show strategies make the difference between the show being an ineffective expense or a proven revenue generator. If you aren't getting tangible results from a show, it's because you didn't plan well or you are at the wrong show (which indicates even poorer planning).

If you are a boat dealer, there's a local or regional show for you. If you are a boat manufacturer, there are national and international shows for you. Don't make the mistake so many other business owners do. They fail to plan and they fail to follow up. Everybody is excited about generating leads, but once they get back to the day-to-day, the leads go stale. Be sure to follow up within a couple of days with the exact information your contacts have asked for.

GAIN WISDOM THROUGH INFORMATION

Leaders are readers and readers are leaders. Wisdom comes from reading. The wiser we become, the better we are able to lead. The better we lead, the more likely it is our businesses will grow. The more our businesses grow, the better able we are to attract great people who can do great things with and for us. That allows you, the business leader, to spend more time gaining even more wisdom. Experts call this a reinforcing loop and I know from personal experience that it works.

If you want to be the leader of a growing business, you need to be an information junkie. Not only should you read the trade publications and reports generated by your industry, you also need to stay current with the changing world in general: locally, regionally, nationally, and even internationally.

I know you don't think you have time for this. I'm urging you to make time, because nothing is more important than gaining wisdom in today's chaotic world.

Chapter 11

Fill Market Vacuums

In the world of capitalism, business creation and business destruction go hand in hand. It's part of the system that new opportunities arise when volatility increases the rate of business failure. You've no doubt already seen some fallout in your industry and community, and it appears that there is still more to come.

For many years, access to cheap capital and a generally rising economic tide created lots of business owners who had no business owning a business. I know that you know who I'm talking about. Maybe it's your neighbor, the former megacorp middle manager, who bought a quick print shop in order to "be her own boss." Or perhaps you perceived it in the seemingly endless stream of new, undercapitalized competitors that were always trying to undercut you. Good times spawned literally millions of business owners who are now learning a tough lesson: Owning a business is never easy.

Conventional wisdom tells us that recessions (and even depressions) offer a great opportunity for an entrepreneurial start-up. Consider this impressive list of examples:

- In August of 1907, 19-year-old Jim Casey and his 18-year-old partner founded the American Messenger Company in Seattle, Washington. In October of that year, a sudden run on a few New York City banks led to what historians now call "The Panic of 1907," which extended across the country. The stock market fell almost 50 percent from its peak the previous year. But that didn't deter Jim and his team. With only $100 of start-up capital and the differentiating slogan, "Best service and lowest rates," the tiny company survived the economic crisis. Today you know that company as United Parcel Service.

- In 1935, friends Bill and Dave graduated together with degrees in electrical engineering, in the middle of the Great Depression. As the decade came to a close and the depression wore on, the two friends partnered in a new venture with $538 of start-up capital. They split the $45-a-month rent for a house that came with a detached garage they soon converted into a workshop. On January 1, 1939, they flipped a coin to determine whose name would come first. Hewlett won over Packard.

- Dennis Brown opened his first motel in Aberdeen, South Dakota, in 1974, a particularly tumultuous year. The Watergate scandal had led to the first resignation of a sitting U.S. President. New president Gerald Ford inherited an expensive conflict in Southeast Asia, plus quadrupling oil prices, a 45 percent drop in the stock market, and an economy mired in "stagflation." Brown countered by setting his room rates at an eye-popping $8.88. By 1977 he was opening a new motel every

18 days. By the time he had gone through the next downturn in the early 1980s, he had franchised in over 250 locations. While today you'll have to pay a bit more than the original $8.88 per night's stay, the Super 8 brand now has over 2,000 locations worldwide.

- Jeff's strategy was out of step with the new high-flyers of the Internet age. While new public offerings soared into the stratosphere with promises of unprecedented returns from the booming economy, Jeff's business plan admitted that reinvestment in the model would mean red ink for years to come. Many investors and pundits laughed at his naiveté. When the dot-com bomb blew up in 2000 and 2001, Jeff stuck to his plan, and he turned his first profit in the fourth quarter of 2001. By January 1, 2009, Jeff Bezos's little company that could, called Amazon.com, had replaced Merrill Lynch on the S&P 100 index, with revenues topping $19 billion annually.

These quintessential stories of the American dream demonstrate that it is possible to persevere in any environment. I've purposely used these examples because the start-ups grew into companies we all know well. I am certain that you too have seen examples of successful recessionary start-ups. In each case the intrepid founder seized the opportunity created by destructive changes. It does happen.

I see and hear people every day who say recessions are a great time to start a business. It makes sense. Commercial real estate prices are depressed. Millions of unemployed workers make it a buyer's market for talent. It's easier to stick out when entrenched competitors are laying low. Potential partners that wouldn't have returned your phone calls are more likely to listen to the optimistic projections of your new entity. For now the laws of supply and demand are creating unusual savings on everything from truck leases to laptops.

I think we can agree that there are a lot of good reasons why downturns create an upside potential for new businesses. However, there are also a host of good reasons to open shop in the middle of an economic boom. I've seen microbusinesses thrive when the macro economy was relatively flat. My point is simply this: The success of any start-up relies more heavily on the acumen and actions of the owner than it does on any specific economic climate.

Regardless of what's happening in the local or national financial environment, the solid foundation of any business depends on the solid performance of the founder or founding partners. While we can never know for sure, I am confident that these overachieving entrepreneurs did not thrive because their companies were founded in a recessionary period; they thrived in spite of it. They did exactly what you need to do. They saw the holes in the market and looked for profitable ways to fill them.

The purpose of your organization is to identify and serve the changing needs of the marketplace. A recession doesn't change that ultimate purpose; it simply changes the nature of the opportunities that are created. This current crisis may be unique in some ways, but it also is much the same as the previous economic storms we have weathered. Attrition and changing market needs are creating vacuums that somebody is going to fill. The question is: Which ones represent the best opportunities for you?

Don't allow a bootstrapping new start-up to fill a void that is rightfully your opportunity. That is easy to say but evidently very hard to do. In every industry in which I've spent any amount of time, established leaders too easily dismiss the brazen new players that seek to fill a small but growing vacuum.

In 1961, Dr. Stanley Pearle opened the first Pearle Vision Center in Savannah, Georgia. Pearle's breakthrough differentiation was simple but profound: one-stop eye care. His retail stores became the first to offer examinations, prescriptions, and glasses in one convenient location. Customers benefited by both the newfound ease and quicker turnaround times (orders could be picked up in just a few days). By 1980, the superior offering had allowed Pearle to become the country's first national player. In 1985 Dr. Pearle sold the company to an international food and beverage conglomerate, Grand Metropolitan Plc, based in London.

LensCrafters was founded in the depths of the recession of the early 1980s, just outside Cincinnati, Ohio. Thirty-eight-year-old founder Dean Butler had learned his marketing skills at Procter and Gamble. His new retail concept was also simple and profound. He met Pearle on their one-stop shopping concept, but differentiated by offering "glasses in about an hour." Because Butler placed his stores in malls, customers could easily fill that hour by shopping and then pick up their glasses before going back to their car.

The concept took off immediately. First-year sales were $2 million. Within four years the concept had been purchased by the powerful U.S. Shoe Corporation and sales exceeded $300 million a year. By 1986 LensCrafters was opening new stores at a rate of two per week.

I was working for Pearle Vision Centers' national advertising agency in 1987, and at the time they were still the only national eye care chain. This division of the big British conglomerate tended to dismiss their upstart rival, LensCrafters, in meetings I attended. As a young account executive, I assumed that the new team of managers could see their competition with a clear eye. As it turned out, they had blinders on. They viewed LensCrafters as a niche player. Besides, Pearle Vision was just coming out of a terrible recession and the economy still appeared shaky at best. They had plenty of real problems to worry about.

By 1992, LensCrafters had passed Pearle Vision to become America's largest eyeglass retail chain. In less than 10 years, they had managed to beat the market leader at their own game. Stanley Pearle, if he had still been in charge, would no doubt have seen the opportunity for meeting the market's growing demand for speed. The managers of the British conglomerate were so focused on their own internal operational issues that they were blinded to the immense opportunity that had built their Pearle Vision brand—greater convenience. They should have realized that people wanted their glasses more quickly. They didn't react until it was too late. Today, the two eyecare chains are owned by the same company (Luxottica Group) and their battle is long over. The fact that both brands are now successfully operating under the same corporate umbrella proves to me that Pearle Vision should have been the first to launch their own segmentation "startup" that filled the market's growing need for even greater speed.

Pearle Vision was the giant that little LensCrafters hit right between the eyes. To you, as a business owner, the lesson here should be crystal clear. Your inability to see opportunity for your business won't be caused by lack of knowledge. Instead, one of your greatest barriers to growth will be knowing so much that you can't see the obvious.

Try to extricate yourself from the shackles of your status quo. Ask yourself this simple question: If we wanted to put ourselves out of business, how would we do it? Don't allow an upstart to show you where the opportunities lie.

In a volatile market like this, no one should have a better chance at a successful "start-up" than you.

Filling market vacuums is about proactively scanning the horizon for unmet needs. Remember: Status quo is the opposite of "grow."

Chapter 12

Partner for Profit

As new opportunities present themselves in the form of market vacuums, one of the most obvious ways to take advantage of those opportunities is to partner with other organizations. While there are many ways in which you can partner, the underlying strategy remains the same. Partnerships can create synergies $(1 + 1 = 3)$ or mitigate potential risks. Sometimes they can do both.

Conventional wisdom on partnering in a recession would make you think that the idea only applies to big business. I have seen and heard very little about it among business owners I've met recently. Yet for all the same reasons it works for big business, common sense says partnering can also put your business in a better position to seize new opportunities.

DISTRIBUTION PARTNERS

Let's say you're the owner of a premium ice cream company. You make hand-crafted, small-batch ice creams in the back of the house and sell them by the scoop, pint, and quart through a front-of-house retail shop. Your business has grown steadily on caramel cashew crunch and mocha chocolate swirl. For years you had all the customers you could handle and then your retail cone sprang a leak. Not everyone can afford premium prices for ice cream when they are having trouble paying their grocery bills.

At your local Chamber of Commerce meeting you are introduced to the owner of a fine dining restaurant who is in a similar fix. You and the owner-chef devise a mutually beneficial partnership. He agrees to prominently feature your brand on his menu in exchange for custom-created seasonal flavors. In one fell swoop (or is that scoop?), you have moved from being solely an ice cream retailer to also being a wholesale provider. Your monthly volume of unique concoctions like pumpkin raisin ice cream and passion fruit sorbet helps cover your overhead costs. The restaurateur now can offer fresh, exclusive, and high-margin new desserts for his patrons. It's the proverbial win-win.

Whether you are a retailer, a business-to-business concern, or a consumer services entity, look for distribution partnerships that are beyond the obvious. Together, you may be dipping into some sweet returns.

PRODUCT AND SERVICE PARTNERSHIPS

I know a technology company that develops software solutions for the institutional food service industry. Despite the recession, their business is steadily and profitably growing. While the owner can point to many legitimate reasons for their success, one has been their increased emphasis on bundling point-of-sale equipment into more software installations. By partnering with a specific equipment manufacturer, they have increased their average customer value while also gaining better control. The old days of trying to get someone else's equipment to interface with their software platform are becoming a thing of the past.

The professional services industry also does a good job of partnering. Most attorneys involved in estate planning partner with accountants and financial planners who also specialize in estates. Real estate agents partner with home inspectors and mortgage brokers. Business that comes into any of the partners spreads to the others.

By the way, remember that there is very little difference between a product and a service. If you are deciding between a whole life and term life insurance policy, you are deciding between two services that have been marketed as products. When you buy sound equipment from a full-service retailer, the components are a given. What differentiates them from the warehouse store is the selection, installation, and guarantee of quick and effective troubleshooting should any problems arise. Everyone needs to think of their business as offering both products and services. Look for partners that strengthen the side where you are weakest.

MARKETING PARTNERSHIPS

In a struggling economy, all owners are looking for more efficient ways to market their business. For example, lately I've noticed an interesting trend. The retailers in struggling strip malls are not financially able to justify broadcast advertising as individual businesses. However, pooling together their limited resources, they can collectively afford a significant local cable and radio schedule that touts their convenient location and wide range of shopping choices. Some even rotate a featured retailer with every spot, because they understand that more traffic for one means more traffic for all. While this tactic is not new, it appears to be much more prevalent in today's challenging retail environment.

Bartering can be a great way to forge a marketing partnership. For instance, if you own a glossy local lifestyle magazine, you could easily trade ads for goods and services. Cash may be king, but you can often get more value out of a noncash transaction, especially if you were going to spend that money anyway.

Let's say your magazine holds two big events a year. You outsource the event's management services to a local firm at the cost of $10,000 a year. The owner of the event management business has hinted that your magazine would be the perfect exposure vehicle for her enterprise, but right now the two-person firm can't afford it. Instead of giving them $10,000 a year, why not give them ten full-page, full-color ads at $1,000 a pop (your full rate card price).

The incremental cost to your magazine for the page is incidental. No, you didn't get $10,000 in, but you didn't pay out the already budgeted $10,000 either. Plus, in this down market, you are getting your full rate card value while everyone else is trying to negotiate your rates down. The owner of the event services company, who couldn't otherwise afford to advertise with you, wins with the prominent display ads.

Fair Warning: While there are lots of reasons why trading goods and services makes sense, not surprisingly, the IRS is fully aware of these types of transactions and has a variety of rules to which you must adhere. The way the IRS sees it, barter dollars are no different from actual dollars. If you barter for another company's products or services, you need to declare the fair market value of anything you "sold" as taxable income.

Marketing partnerships in the consumer world are easier to describe, yet the opportunities for business-to-business marketing partnerships are equally viable. After speaking at a national logistics industry conference, I walked the trade show floor to see and hear what was happening in the industry. I met the inventor and marketer of a successful three-year-old gizmo. He split the cost of the exhibit space with his much larger manufacturing partner, who had no previous interest in the logistics industry. The gizmo company owner and the big manufacturer's representative agreed it was a great investment in time and money for both partners.

PRICING PARTNERSHIPS

As we have already learned, pricing is one of the most important aspects of marketing. Imagine you are the owner of a 4-star boutique hotel in a major metropolitan area. By partnering with a last-minute Internet travel booking site, you can offer a discounted deal through the consolidator to effectively fill rooms below your regular published rate. This helps you keep your price integrity, while filling rooms that would otherwise have stayed empty. If you are profitable at 60 percent occupancy, getting to 80 percent through this third party helps cash flow directly to your bottom line. Airlines, cruise ships, rental car companies, and tour operators use this strategy all the time, and so could you.

Pricing partnerships can also help you generate volume. Let's say you're the owner of an efficiency consultancy firm, and an association of process control engineers approaches you with a partnership idea. The association wants to provide their members with affordable on-site evaluations. You agree this is a perfect fit for your business. The price you are charging the association for a guaranteed number of engagements is a bit lower than your "one-off" daily rate. Yet the known fees generated will help you better manage everything from your cash flow to your consultants' calendars.

STRATEGIC ALLIANCES

A strategic alliance is a more formalized partnership that usually implies a greater commitment by the parties

involved in terms of time, money, and effort. Both players have a piece of the puzzle that fits together. For example, rather than trying to figure out how to sell into
India, you instead find someone to become your agent
because they know the lay of the land and the peculiar-
ities of the market. It's their job to take your product or
service and translate its benefits to meet local needs. This
could be an independent sales representative, an established company whose customer base is similar to yours,
or a specialty distributor you haven't done business with
before.

As I mentioned earlier, I was once the president of a
small manufacturing company that produced safety products. Hard hats were our specialty. We were approached
by another, much larger manufacturer of safety products
who had recently won a multi-year contract to supply a
complete occupational safety solution for an international
company's manufacturing facilities. We were able to en-
ter into a contracted strategic alliance, providing a private
label program for the larger player. For our partner, this
was a small but necessary detail. For us, it was an enormous opportunity. This successful arrangement opened
our eyes to other such alliances.

Soon afterward, we identified an opportunity to offer
our customers so-called fashionable eye protection. The
cost for us to retool and manufacture these increasingly
popular products was prohibitive. I soon found myself
standing in a converted chicken coop in southern Taiwan

entering into a strategic alliance with a similarly sized company who wanted to break into the U.S. market. This too proved to be a mutually beneficial relationship.

JOINT VENTURES

Many people use the terms "strategic alliance" and "joint venture" interchangeably. There is an important distinction. A joint venture actually creates, legally, a new entity.

A few years ago I worked with a regional producer of in-home coupon circulars. Her primary expertise was helping local businesses generate first-time trial, from muffler shops to roofers to fast food franchisees. At a point, she realized that printing was not only her greatest cost, but it had grown to well over a million dollars a year. Her business was not too adversely affected by the economic downturn following the events of September 11, 2001. However, she had a friend who owned a small printing operation that had been profitable but was now really struggling.

The partners pulled together his printing expertise and her volume to create a new venture. Together, they leased some low-cost commercial space in a warehouse district and co-signed a note with an equipment leasing company for the new equipment. Her volume alone covered their costs, including the veteran sales representative hired to find other printing jobs. In little more than a year, the venture was profitable. Today the revenue generated by the new venture has eclipsed the original entities' sales at the beginning of the partnership. She says that thanks to the powerful joint venture, they are now "printing money for a living."

Chapter 13

Pursue Potential Acquisitions

Caveat emptor.   —Latin for *Let the buyer beware*

■ ■ ■

I talk to hundreds of business owners every month. When I ask veteran owners the question, "Are you finding any opportunities in this recession?" there is one most common answer: "Yes—acquisition!" The conventional wisdom among business owners is that this downturn will be "temporary." Weaker players appear particularly vulnerable to owners with access to capital. The stronger entrepreneur rightly sees this as an opportunity to pounce. I agree, *if* you know what you are doing.

Bobby Albert is the owner of Albert Moving, based in Wichita Falls, Texas. The company was founded by his father during the Great Depression. Bobby took the helm in August, 1973, just in time for another steep economic downturn. At that point, the company's total annual revenues were about $100,000. By moving slowly but surely, Bobby built the business to more than $2 million in revenue by 1987. In that same year, Albert Moving made its first strategic acquisition—a smaller local player that easily fit into their existing framework. While the purchase ultimately proved successful, it also provided Bobby with some valuable lessons on what works and what doesn't in the art of acquisition.

After successfully completing the first one, Bobby saw a continuing growth opportunity. Over the last 12 years he put together five additional acquisitions. One helped gain a foothold in the truck rental business. Others allowed him to offer records management and information destruction services. Two others allowed him to improve his position in the packing, loading, and unloading side of the business. Today Albert Moving is a growing $25 million+ a year business providing moving services to families, businesses, and the military.

Let me stop this story for a moment and be perfectly clear that Albert Moving is not a customer of mine. While I have spoken to Bobby Albert on the phone and met with him face-to-face, I was the student and he was the teacher. I have orchestrated a few small deals in my time, but my experience was preschool stuff compared to Bobby's PhD-level work.

He maintains that the secret to growth through acquisition is looking for not only a tight strategic fit, but also for an even tighter cultural alignment. Bobby and his full-time team of three acquisition experts are always on the lookout for a new perfect fit. Over the last few years there have been plenty of opportunities that looked good on paper, but he and his team have learned how to truly assess a deal. For Albert Moving, due diligence goes well beyond balance sheets and profit & loss statements. "If it's not a strategic fit and a cultural fit, we know to walk away," Bobby says. "We're not interested in buying somebody else's problems." As a result, no matter how things look initially, they pass on the majority of deals that come their way.

The value of an acquisition should always be more than the projected revenue stream. Anyone can crunch the financials and make a case for buying any business at a given price. The greatest lesson I learned from Bobby Albert was when he told me, "I'm not really a financial guy. I've just developed a good sense now for what fits our business." Bobby is a modest man, and I'm certain that he is actually pretty astute when it comes to the financial side of the equation. However, experience has taught him that there is much more to be factored into any deal than simply money. After 12 years of buying and absorbing other companies, he has become an acquisition expert.

There's no question that opportunities to acquire other businesses will look particularly attractive in today's uncertain economy. In such volatile times, however, I have two critical questions for you: (1) Are you an acquisition expert? (2) Have you ever managed even one acquisition deal before? If the answer to both questions is no, then I urge you to proceed with the utmost caution. It's rarely as simple as it seems.

For many years I've worked with Bill Binder, second generation owner and first class operator of Candlewic, a national manufacturer and distributor of candle supplies for the crafting industry. I first met Bill in the midst of the recession following 9/11. With a bit of my input, Bill was able to turn his manufacturing-driven company into a truly customer-driven marketing machine. In 2003, Bill called me to discuss a tremendous new opportunity.

A smaller company that had a line of soap making supplies wanted to get out of the industry. Bill knew that candle making and soap making were closely aligned in the minds of crafting enthusiasts. You don't have to be an expert to see why. Both crafts involve pouring hot liquids enhanced with a wide variety of colors and fragrances into shaping molds. Bill's own internal research showed that 30 percent of his customers were also soap makers. The soap making company was also known for its strong line of packaged retail products, an area in which Bill hoped to expand further.

On paper, this looked like a perfect fit. Bill figured that the acquisition would increase his sales by 20 percent in the first year alone.

Once the two parties had agreed on an asset purchase deal, Bill entered into a thorough due diligence process. The soap maker's top customers had a long track record of loyalty and represented greater strength for Candlewic in attractive geographies. In addition to the new customers, Bill was also acquiring valuable inventory. The soap maker wanted out. Bill wanted in. This was a no-brainer!

So often, when two owners reach an agreement in principle, both parties feel like they are close to closing the deal. Once the attorneys get involved, however, these things always take considerably longer than either party anticipates (especially if the attorneys are being paid by the hour).

For Bill Binder, the first sign of potential trouble came during the closing phase. The repeatedly delayed closing date ended up falling into peak season for both companies. The acquired company had little incentive to fully service their soon-to-be ex-customers, and inventory levels were not being fully replenished. Once the deal was consummated, the inventory received at Candlewic was incomplete and disorganized. Valuable new customers, already on backorder, were now clamoring for delivery. While Candlewic was busy trying to sort through unmarked vials of citrus oils and colored dyes, impatient customers were beginning to defect.

Other unanticipated problems further exasperated the situation. Candlewic employees were slower to embrace soap than Bill had expected. While some of the bigger customers were willing to work with a new vendor, there were greater than expected defections from the mid-tier buyers. The initial sales projections were also undercut by an overall decline in the crafting industry. Bill's glowing opportunity was in jeopardy of becoming a meltdown.

Bill Binder has learned a tough but valuable lesson. Today, Candlewic still offers soap supplies. Yet sales and synergies have failed to approach the initial targets. Bill says, "The product line may someday reach its expected potential, but at this point in time it has not." While

Candlewic's acquisition certainly can't be described as a failure, the question remains, "Was it all worth it?" What other compelling opportunities were given less attention during this period?

Bill now understands the problem with most acquisitions. Rarely do you get exactly what you think you are getting. No-brainers simply don't exist. No matter how perfect it looks on paper or how much due diligence you conduct, unforeseeable problems are the norm, not the exception. Acquisitions do represent a tremendous opportunity in a recession. If you are walking on firm financial ground, you should be on the lookout for a good one. Just be certain that you look beyond the financial fit and be absolutely sure that there is a strategic and cultural fit as well.

Like Bobby Albert, Bill Binder now has the experience to consider another acquisition. If you haven't done one before, you don't. But of course we all have to start somewhere. If an acquisition opportunity comes knocking at your door, don't get so emotionally invested that you lose sight of the necessary time, money and effort you will invest in order to make it work.

The common sense approach to acquisitions is simple: *caveat emptor* or "Let the buyer beware."

Chapter 14

Put Better Tools to Work

Anthropologists have always defined the human condition by the use of tools.

I don't know your religious beliefs and I certainly don't want to step on them, but anthropologists now believe that tool-using Homo sapiens with opposable thumbs have been on this Earth for 200,000 years, give or take a millennium. There's been a Stone Age, a Bronze Age, an Iron Age, and an Industrial Age. You and I now live in an Information Age. New tools have always mattered in the progress of industry and commerce, and they matter more today than ever before. How you choose to put the tools of our time to work creates opportunity, because the tools of our time can both make us money and save us money. Today's tools are powerful.

The conventional wisdom I am hearing these days says to make do with less; in other words, try your best to put off capital expenditures for new tools until business gets better. But when it comes to the tools of our time, I say try to do *more for less* instead. Employee retention, customer satisfaction, and overall efficiency have to be factored into your equation. When you have an opportunity to invest in better tools that more than pay for themselves in a timely manner, you can't afford not to do it.

Your existing tools don't know there's a recession, and greater efficiency is more important than ever in a downturn. No one can allow mission-critical tools go down. If you're a metal stamper, you're literally out of business if your stamper isn't stamping. A deli with a malfunctioning meat slicer, a hairstylist with a blown blow-dryer, or a drywall hanger with a jammed nail gun are similarly disadvantaged. Obviously, the tools that directly relate to the delivery of your product or service need to function at all times. If you don't invest in maintenance and necessary replacements, you're going to miss opportunities. Indeed, our tools have the habit of breaking down when we need them most.

There are other tools on which we depend, despite the fact that they don't directly produce revenue. Anything in your business can be made more efficient with better tools, from your office operations to your financial processes to your sales and marketing efforts.

There is nothing more frustrating for your employees than an important tool that doesn't work well or doesn't work at all. A constantly malfunctioning copy machine can be the last straw for a valuable employee.

How old are the information technology tools in your organization? Many business owners are shocked to discover that the desktop office computer or point-of-sale system they "just bought" is actually approaching its fourth anniversary. You don't need to be on the bleeding edge, but putting yourself on the leading edge of information technology translates into a clear differentiator: speed. This is especially true if your competitors are ignoring their own obvious need for upgraded tools.

Important business tools are cheaper than ever before. Tool providers are discounting everything from fuel-efficient delivery vans to faster, cheaper, and better multimedia laptops. Chances are any tool that would make you more efficient is now more affordable. Also, the experts who know how to put tools to work are looking for work. There are bargains to be had on installation and training right now too.

Uncle Sam has also created incentives for you to invest in tools. Recent changes to the tax code allow you to accelerate deductions on new machinery, computers, vehicles, and other capital equipment. No telling how long this "bonus depreciation" window will be left open, but now is a good time to invest in new tools if you need them.

Some of the best things in life are free, or pretty close to it. It's not hard to calculate the return on investment with these tools:

Basic website hosting with Microsoft Live	FREE
PayPal merchant account (basic)	FREE
Survey Monkey's online surveys system	FREE
Blogging software and hosting from Wordpress or Blogger	FREE
QuickBooks Simple Start accounting software	FREE
GoToMyPC remote desktop access	$15 per month
1-800 phone number with virtual fax	$10 per month

When it comes to the tools of our time, I have one particular pet peeve. Over the past decade, web sites have become proven tools in almost every industry. Unfortunately, most business owners have failed to reap the rewards. A 2009 study by Nielsen and Webvisible found that only 44 percent of small businesses in the United States have a web site. That number seems pretty low to me, but it is almost beside the point. The true lost opportunity here is that the web sites I see are so ineffectual. Most, whether they are consumer or business-to-business, represent little more than outdated brochures. How often have you pulled up a company's web site and not been able to find something that should obviously be there? Restaurant sites without menus, hotel sites without their current rates, group medical practice sites with no ability to make an appointment. To me, these obvious omissions are inexcusable.

However, my greatest concern is lost revenue opportunities. I recently conducted a workshop for a group of owners specializing in industrial equipment distribution. About two-thirds of the way through our day together, I mentioned that I had visited most of their web sites and was surprised to find that on many I couldn't buy anything. There was plenty of information about the long upstanding history of the companies, plus pretty pictures of their employees and facilities. I could even peruse the particularly wide range of products they carried. I just couldn't buy one.

No sooner had I expressed my opinion than a couple of hands shot up in the air. "I appreciate the feedback, Steve, but I don't think you understand our business very well," one said. "Most of the products we ship are customized."

"We asked our customers if they wanted to buy through our web site and they said no," said another.

I was surprised to be debating something that seemed so obvious. I pushed back a little, suggesting that at least replacement parts could be sold more efficiently through a web interface. The most vocal skeptics and I agreed to disagree and we simply moved on. I even admitted it was possible their industry really was different and left it at that.

Later that night at dinner, I was approached by no less than three owners who had kept quiet earlier in the day. In effect, all three whispered in my ear, "Hey, you're absolutely right about web sites. We've been making a killing selling parts online lately. I just didn't want my competitors in the room to hear about it."

I can't imagine a business where a well-conceived, interactive web site can't be an affordable differentiator. For the owners of those distributorships that believe their customers don't want to buy parts online, their assumption becomes a self-fulfilling prophecy. Many customers are buying replacement parts online; they're just not buying from them.

A twenty-first-century organization that doesn't fully avail itself of the efficiencies and opportunities created by better tools is, in effect, building its own barriers to growth. Go put the tools of your time to work and find the opportunities in them.

Chapter 15

Green is Growing

It wasn't very long ago that many industries and companies viewed "green" initiatives as representing anything *but* opportunities. Today, business owners from the construction trades to consumer packaging companies recognize sustainable systems as being synonymous with good business practices.

There are plenty of good reasons for making your business more green. From reducing dependence on foreign oil to ensuring cleaner land, water, and skies for future generations, organizations like yours are rapidly adopting more sustainable business processes in an effort to become more socially responsible. However, there is another compelling argument for these new ways of working that is often overlooked: Companies like yours are discovering that green can also mean gold.

In the interest of full disclosure, it's important to state clearly that I consider myself to be a political agnostic and a business growth realist. I'll let the media, lobbyists, and elected officials struggle to define the current state of climate change or future carbon emission standards. In the meantime, I see a huge opportunity for you in today's business climate. How will you meet this emerging opportunity?

It's important to consider that your customers' attitudes have already shifted. I've seen surveys where nearly 90 percent of consumers report a preference for doing business with companies committed to "environmentally-friendly practices." Even if your organization is engaged in foreign trade or business-to-business activities, I believe it's safe to assume that your customers increasingly weigh their perception of your company's social responsibility when making purchase decisions. Indeed, the debate about the importance of eco-friendly behavior is effectively closed. If your company is seen as the proverbial ostrich with its head in the sand, you risk falling behind competitors that are considered more responsive to today's real and perceived environmental challenges.

The economic rewards of becoming more energy efficient have moved from "nice to do" to "need to do." While the pain of oil at $140 per barrel has eased, a price spike could easily happen again when the world economy picks up. The long-term trend of rising worldwide demand for energy, combined with growing concern about global climate change, compels us to prioritize true efficiency as never before. Shifting consumer attitudes and volatile commodities pricing should be viewed as both daunting challenges and ripe opportunities. I believe that by the year 2020, when we look back at this pivotal moment in time, it will be the business leaders who had a 20/20 vision of this new reality who will have achieved sustainable and profitable growth.

PrintingForLess.com, based in Livingston, Montana, is one of the nation's fastest growing commercial printers.

Company founder and president Andrew Field believes that a focus on environmental responsibility throughout their production process leads to both higher quality and lower cost printing for their customers. Their inks are all vegetable-based. Their paper is milled chlorine-free with all pulp harvested in a sustainable manner; 100 percent of their electricity is created by a nearby "windmill farm." They package with biodegradable padding materials instead of petroleum-based foam "peanuts."

According to PFL director of manufacturing Wyeth Windham, these initiatives offer another money-making component: They help the company retain its employees. As he says, "The best and the brightest demand environmental consciousness in their workplace. They need to know that the work they do won't accelerate the melting of the polar ice caps. Now that's a retention tool!"

To start your move from green to gold, ask yourself these five questions:

1. What can I do right away that will have little or no cost but will be highly valued by my employees, customers, and community?

2. What new products and services can I develop that will meet the changing demands of a greener marketplace in the near-term future?

3. Which of my current processes, policies, and work-flows made sense during times of cheaper energy and

commodities but should now be reevaluated for their overall cost and environmental impact?

4. What longer-term, more capital-intensive projects do I need to budget for in order to reduce long-term energy consumption and costly waste?

5. How can I best monitor the opportunities created by the changing political environment at the federal, state and local level?

Here's one last word of advice. The best way to be perceived as greener is to actually be greener. Most people will ultimately see through any attempts at bogus "greenwashing." Like most everything associated with business growth opportunities, authenticity is key to sustainable success.

Chapter 16

Catch a Falling Star

For many years, the greatest barrier to growth for privately held businesses in this country was their inability to find enough skilled workers. Throughout the current decade, analysts and economists, from the U.S. Bureau of Labor Statistics to the Conference Board, were sounding the shortage alarm. Many experts were forecasting a 10 million shortfall by 2010 and 20 million missing workers by 2020. It was *the* issue for any business owner hoping to climb to the next level.

By 2008, however, things began to fall off a cliff. By January 2009, 3.6 million jobs had been lost since the start of the recession (officially December 2007), with nearly half of the decline occurring in just the previous three months. These losses were now coming from all over the country and across nearly all major employment sectors. So much for the labor shortage, right?

Honestly, I don't know for sure, and neither does any economist or government analyst. You could guess, I suppose, but what is the point? No one knows where this is headed. Will we reach the 25 percent unemployment figures of the Great Depression? Will the massive government spending keep unemployment below the 1980–82 recessionary levels of 10.8 percent?

For years conventional wisdom told us that we were going to have a labor shortage. Now, with jobless figures ballooning, does this thinking still make sense? While I don't have a crystal ball, my common sense tells me this is a rare opportunity. In fact, I believe this is your greatest opportunity of all. Highly skilled, proven performers are either on the street or soon will be. I don't mean pretty good; I mean truly great people—the falling stars—who are suddenly within your reach. You have an opportunity to grab one.

Regardless of how quickly the economy recovers or how many unemployed workers we have, the key for you is to concentrate on the word "skilled," not "worker." In the twenty-first century, highly skilled people are going to continue to be rare and valuable. Five years from now, we are going to see this moment in time as an anomaly, a temporary blip. The giant macro forces of demographic shifts and a knowledge-based economy are still going to be with us. *As a business owner, you are being presented with the rare opportunity to participate in a temporary buyer's market for talent.*

Most business owners see hiring as an unpleasant chore. In a recession they see it as unnecessary chore. If you are considering letting people go or have already started, it can be hard to remember that business leaders are always in the market for superior people.

Finding the best and the brightest should never be a sudden event. Even in tough times, the future of your business depends on your being in recruitment mode at all times. Recruitment doesn't keep you from your real job. This *is* your real job. Only now, thanks to there being so many fallen stars available, that job has become an even higher priority. Even if you only have a staff of two, ask yourself what one prudent superstar could mean to your chances for success.

Both conventional wisdom and common sense should be telling you that this is a good time to upgrade the overall quality of your team. However, you have to approach this opportunity with a clear head and a well-devised strategy. Below are some of the supposed truisms you are probably hearing right now. Like so many generalities, there is at least a grain of truth in each one, but for your specific situation, consider whether they truly apply.

NOW IS A GREAT TIME TO HIRE BECAUSE SO MANY MORE PEOPLE ARE LOOKING FOR A JOB

There's no doubt about it, plenty of people are looking for work right now. Recently I talked to a Florida client who ran an ad for an $11-an-hour general office worker. The business was inundated with 200 resumes the following day. An old friend of mine owns a hazardous materials cleaning company in a midwestern state. His business is growing, he needs quality workers, and he is willing to pay well above local wage scales to get them. Unfortunately, over half of the people they actually interview flunk a basic literacy test and/or a controlled substance test.

Remember, quantity does not necessarily mean quality. Sorting through a lot of rocks right now can make it difficult to find the true diamonds.

MORE PEOPLE WITH EXPERIENCE IN YOUR INDUSTRY HAVE BECOME AVAILABLE

Whatever industry you are in, chances are the ranks of the unemployed have increased. It is also pretty likely that there are plenty of people trying to jump from a leaky ship competitor. If a proven sales professional with a stellar reputation in your industry asks for an interview, make it happen. However, don't just hire her based on her past performance and contacts. If an applicant doesn't fit your unique culture, you're both going to lose.

In the recession of the early 1990s, my bigger competitors were all "rightsizing," while we began growing and therefore hiring. I considered dozens of my competitors' sales, operations, and financial staffers. In the end I hired only one. Usually a simple phone conversation helped me better understand why the applicant was no longer with my competitor. Their resumes made them sound like falling stars, but they were really fading castoffs.

Organizations of any size will do anything to keep their superstars. Be quick to address any approach from competitors' former and current personnel. You'll always learn something. However, be very slow to actually pull the trigger.

MORE PEOPLE WITH A SPECIFIC SKILL SET YOU ARE LACKING ARE AVAILABLE

I was recently forwarded an e-mail from a company looking for a candidate who met the following requirements: "Must have a BSME or BSEE degree or preferably a Masters Degree, plus 10+ years of experience handling major accounts in the electromechanical devices area, i.e.: solenoids, flap actuations, switch subsystems, and micro motors."

Are they serious? Someone this specific is either the person who left them or the person they are competing with. If this kind of specificity is actually required, they should already have been in contact with the few stars that fit the bill, long before the need arose.

In almost all cases, I reject the notion that such tight qualifications would best serve your interests. Surely a proven quota-busting sales professional with an engineering background can be quickly taught the unique selling proposition of this company's "flap actuations." Scanning the whole sky is the best way to spot falling stars, not pointing your telescope at one specific constellation.

Great people are capable of great things. Look for proven winners because they have learned how to win.

Instead of specific skills and education, identify exception-ally bright, goal-oriented team players who have demon-strated an ability to adapt to changing environments. If that person happens to meet your exact qualifications wish list, so be it.

PEOPLE ARE WILLING TO TAKE LESS WHEN TIMES ARE TOUGH

Yes, in an economic crisis candidates are more likely to accept a lower offer. But what happens when things pick up? In my experience, people do what they have to do to survive economic downturns. However, they never forget what they used to be paid.

Even if you convince someone to take a cut, they will always be looking for ways to get back to where they were. It's simply human nature. Be it five months or five years from now when things turn around, they're going to be looking for you to make them whole again. If you can't do it, they'll eventually find someone who can.

When the person in front of you is saying that lower compensation is acceptable, show them that there is a plausible path for getting back to where they were. Right now, it may serve both parties' interests to start at a lower base. If the applicants are truly stars, they will rise to the occasion if you present them with challenging but achievable goals.

BIG BUSINESS STARS ARE POUNDING THE PAVEMENT

When publicly held companies lay off thousands at a time, they tend to throw out the good with the bad. If you've ever wished you could afford someone with a specific skill set—a Six Sigma black belt, a Cordon Bleu chef, or a C++ programmer for instance—maybe now you can.

The best manager I ever hired in my life came from a big multinational corporation. At one time he managed over a thousand people. I knew I wanted him and had been actively recruiting him for a couple of years. When the recession of the early 1990s hit and his group was cut in half, he was suddenly calling me. On paper it looked like we couldn't afford him. Within a year he was more than paying for himself.

In the recession of 2002, a client of mine was struggling to make an expensive new factory automation software work for his business. The much larger automation software vendor started having trouble during the downturn. The smaller but growing manufacturer was able to hire the same person who had trained his people on the system to come in and manage it every day. It turned out to be a big win for this small business owner.

There is no question that some people can make the transition from big business to small business. In my experience, however, this is the exception rather than the rule. Two-thirds of people who work in big business say they would prefer to work in a smaller business. Yet the first time they find themselves taping up their own overnight shipment or taking out the break room garbage, they often wonder what they have gotten themselves into.

Generally speaking, I have found that people who have previously succeeded in smaller, privately held businesses are the ones most likely to succeed in another similarly sized privately held business. I also believe you shouldn't accept generalizations about anything these days, especially when it comes to proven people.

Chapter 17

Train the Talented

All of us do not have equal talents, but all of us should have an equal opportunity to develop our talents.
*—*John F. Kennedy

∎   ∎   ∎

People are our greatest asset. Have you heard this one before? Is it currently plastered on your web site and your sales materials?

If somebody were ever to build the Hollow Business Phrase Hall of Fame, this one would stand right up there with "Your call is very important to us." Everyone says these truisms because they make sense. Yet when times get tough, too many businesses abandon investment in their people.

For many years studies and surveys have shown that business leaders recognize the value of training. But you don't need me to regurgitate these consistent findings in order to tell you something you already know is true. Developing your employees should never be viewed as a cost center. Like marketing communications, when done properly, it is a directly measurable investment in your business's future success.

Devoting the appropriate resources in order to enhance the skill sets of your workforce helps your business in many ways. Bettering your employees betters your chances for innovative thinking, employee retention, and ultimately, sustainable and profitable growth.

Conventional wisdom regarding training in a recession says it's too important to cut off with a tourniquet. Unfortunately, many business owners are forced to do it anyway. I maintain that their behavior is one of survival instinct. They know it's only a short-term cash flow fix, but they believe that they have no choice. Therein lies your opportunity for a long-term competitive advantage.

I have a problem with the word "training." The concept is so general it doesn't really mean anything. I am concerned that many business owners focus their training investment in the wrong areas. I call it push-button training: "Here's how you push the button on the machine to make it work. Here's how you push the button on the computer to produce the report. Here's how you push the button on the phone system to transfer a call." Too often training means teaching new hires how to work with your internal processes. Obviously, some of this is necessary, but it's not your best opportunity. Here's your real training opportunity.

Be sure that both new and existing hires are steeped in customer-driven training. What satisfies your customers or potential customers is never obvious. The people who work with and for you need training systems that continuously teach them what really matters. The answers to the following questions are what effective employees really need to know.

- Why do people buy from us?
- When people buy from our competitors, why do they do it?
- What makes this business unique?
- What do our customers and potential customers care about the most?
- What are the primary tasks we need to know in order to deliver on total customer satisfaction?
- After I've mastered the primary tasks related to my specific job, is there an opportunity to cross-train on other tasks that ensure better customer experiences?

When you can answer these questions, and train other people on them, you will have a distinct competitive advantage.

Here's another training opportunity.

After speaking at a recent event, I got a phone call the next day from a real go-getter. After a successful career in real estate, he had been forced to take a sales job with a local manufacturing company. The $30 million privately held business produced a variety of fabricated metal products. As low man on the totem pole, Mr. Go-Getter was given responsibility for a new and relatively small product with annual sales of about half a million dollars. Through innovative new distribution and marketing communication strategies, he had quadrupled annual sales to more than $2 million in only two years. But Mr. Go-Getter had a problem.

In his most recent review, the business owner and the salesman's direct boss congratulated him on the revenue increase, but told him that his product was falling well short of their profitability targets. He had expected hearty slaps on the back and instead was befuddled to learn that he had somehow fallen short of expectations. His question for me was a simple one: "How should I raise my prices?" After probing a bit further, it became clear to me that he was asking the wrong question.

Mr. Go-Getter thinks of himself as a salesperson, but clearly he is really a product manager. If he already had the authority to change distribution strategies, advertising initiatives, and now pricing structures, his real job in the organization was obviously much broader than simply sales. When told that his profitability was not meeting expectations, he had no choice but to accept the judgment because he had no idea how it was being calculated. He e-mailed me a copy of the profit and loss statement he was handed in his review. The more questions I asked about it, the more I realized he had no idea how to read it, let alone use it. For him it was like looking at two pages of hieroglyphics. This was an opportunity that was screaming for training.

Think about how much more value this potential all-star would bring to his organization with even a smidgen of new skills. I encouraged him to find a training course on business-to-business product management, or financial management for non-financial managers. For a few hundred dollars and a week's worth of time, Mr. Go-Getter could move from passenger to pilot with this high-flying product. Given the knowledge of basic cost accounting, he would be much more likely to navigate his product toward an even greater profit than the arbitrarily set goal. They're asking him to win at a game in which he doesn't even know how to keep score. The only solution here is for our go-getter to go get some much-needed outside training.

One more thing about training. No matter how hard I've tried in the past, there are two things for which I can't really train: innate problem-solving ability and general pleasantness. I can't train someone to be smart and I can't train someone to be nice. I can improve their acumen on specific skills, and I can increase their respect for other people to a degree. However, it is always better to train smart, pleasant people to do their jobs better. People who struggle with learning have trouble grasping what you need them to know. People who don't have good interpersonal skills can improve those skills, but they rarely approach the level of "great." Never settle for less than potentially great people.

Recently, I was sitting in the New Orleans airport. My flight was delayed and I opened my laptop to answer some e-mails. Over the course of the next hour, I witnessed greatness that no amount of training can instill. A young man was given the job of getting five wheelchair-bound seniors through security and to the gate where I was sitting. In every instance, the seniors were somewhat disoriented and they were taking it out on the young man. He could have ignored them. He could have even thrown unpleasantness right back at them. Instead, even though he wasn't aware that anyone was watching, he chose to be great.

Unbeknownst to the young man, I was watching closely. He smiled a lot. When he addressed the seniors, he always came around to the front of their chairs and spoke in an easy to understand, but not condescending, tone. He asked them if they were happy and if there was anything else he could do to make them more comfortable. When he left them to gather another senior, he always assured the one he was leaving that he would be right back to check on him or her.

After watching him marshal five seniors through security, I noticed he had not been tipped at all. Not once. While it is quite possible that a loved one had handled the tipping at check-in, I don't think it would have mattered. In fact, if he had been tipped already, there was no longer an incentive for him to go above and beyond as he did. He was just naturally great. As he walked away for the last time, I chased after the young man and gave him his well-deserved tip. I told him that he had earned it and asked him one simple question: Did your company train you to be so respectful to these seniors?

The young man laughed and said in a distinct New Orleans accent, "No sir, my family taught me to always be nice to older folks. I just pretend they're family no matter how crabby they get. Believe me, this group was nothin' compared to one of my aunties. Besides, these folks are really nice people on the inside, they just have a hard time showin' it sometimes."

In this instance, a young person from one ethnic group had been treated shabbily by five members of another ethnic group, in a city where ethnic tension can run high. Rather than becoming an uncaring robot, the young man made a conscious decision to always treat other people's family members with dignity and respect. I wish I could have hired him on the spot. You and I can't train for that kind of greatness.

Be sure that your training always targets the truly talented. If your people aren't uniquely qualified with both minds and manners, training will be a constant struggle.

Chapter 18

Revisit the Rules

Without continual growth and progress, such words as improvement, achievement, and success have no meaning.

— Benjamin Franklin

■ ■ ■

If you have made it to this point in the book, I trust that your business is weathering the current crisis and you are preparing for a period of profitable growth in the future. To achieve sustainable growth, you need a system (the cause) that produces desirable growth (the effect).

By my definition, companies that are growth leaders achieve sustained increases in revenue and profits of 20 percent or greater for at least five years in a row. I have dedicated my career to understanding how these growth companies manage to do everything better than most others. What do they do differently from other businesses that don't grow, or even fail? Where do the leaders of these organizations devote the most time, money, and effort?

I addressed these questions in detail in my first book, *The 7 Irrefutable Rules of Small Business Growth* (John Wiley & Sons, 2005). While meeting, consulting, and speaking with literally thousands of business growth leaders every year since, I've heard enough success stories to know that those irrefutable rules still apply. They're not irrefutable because I say they are, but rather because owners and leaders of sustained growth organizations never disagree with them.

There are no silver bullets or 17-point checklists that will lead to certain growth. Indeed, I can't tell you *what* to do in order to grow your particular company. However, I can suggest to you *where* organizations like yours should focus their resources. It's within these seven specific areas that sustained growth companies look for the innovations, evolutions, and revolutions that lead to growth, no matter the industry in which they compete nor economic environment to which they must adapt.

STRONG SENSE OF PURPOSE

Just as successful countries, families, and communities all have a strong sense of purpose, so too do most growth organizations. Why are you in business? What truly matters about your company? What is important to you and those that work with and for you? Literally, what gets you and your team out of bed in the morning?

For growth companies, it's never only about money. Money is a great way to keep score, but there must be a greater purpose than simply wealth creation. Business growth leaders consistently set a strong sense of purpose for their company, and it always permeates throughout the organization. They create a distinct culture that answers the question, "What really matters around here?"

OUTSTANDING MARKET INTELLIGENCE

We all need a macro view of the marketplace. If you want to grow, you must be able to first recognize, and then adapt to, fundamental changes in your company, your community, and your industry.

In general, smaller businesses are pretty good at managing internal issues—order flow, office procedures, phone response time, or similar internal measuring sticks. However, we are often too myopic. Heads down in our day-to-day activities, we are unable to see the important outside forces of change that will shape our business. Big businesses are often the opposite. While having a good handle on external forces of change, the left hand and the right hand don't always work in concert within the organization.

When it comes to your focus, there is no right or wrong. Instead, it is the balance of the two that leads to growth, regardless of the organization's size. Keeping your internal processes humming while simultaneously monitoring the outside forces of change is essential for future growth.

EFFECTIVE GROWTH PLANNING

In my experience, organizations that have sustained growth are much more likely to have an effective growth planning system in place. In order to be effective, the plan must be written, well-communicated, and regularly updated. While not the most important of the seven rules described here, this one is the best predictor of sustained growth.

The most effective growth plans I've seen are not fill-in-the-blank boilerplates or printouts from wizard-driven software packages. Instead, they are usually homegrown systems that reflect that particular organization's unique needs. The leaders of such an organization decide what the plan is to be called, when it will be updated, and what information it will include. The best plans start at the bottom and percolate up to the top; they are not decrees from on high. When employees see it as "management's" plan, it may cause pushback from within the organization. When it's developed as "our" plan, there is a much higher likelihood of success.

One more thing on plans: the shorter the better. It is easy to throw together a 50-page document about everything everyone knows and thinks and wants. It is a much more arduous task to get your plan down to its pithy essentials. I recommend 15 pages at a maximum. When you get really good, you'll be able to get it down to five pages.

CUSTOMER-DRIVEN PROCESSES

Every business is a series of people carrying out processes. Unfortunately, as we grow, these processes can tend to serve the organization at the expense of the customer. Take a look at all your processes from a customer's perspective. Are your systems built to make the organization's life easier, or do they serve to make a customer's experience, and thereby allegiance, better?

To be truly customer-driven, any process that touches a customer needs to integrate the best thinking from your entire organization. Find out what your customers really want you to concentrate on, then do those things better than anyone else. Warning: the processes that actually matter the most are rarely intuitive. Look for ways to define and deliver on "better" better.

THE POWER OF TECHNOLOGY

In earlier chapters we touched on tools and technology as they relate to efficiency and doing more for less. But tools also define who we are and what we can accomplish, impacting our potential for growth in the future.

We do live in an Information Age. How you choose to put the tools of your time to work will have a significant impact on your business and its chances for sustained growth. Better tools can help your business improve your marketing, internal operations, office administration, hiring practices, and nearly any other process that impacts your ultimate success.

Keep your eyes open for new tools that can give you a competitive edge and help your business grow. If you're in business, you are in the technology business—no exceptions.

THE BEST AND BRIGHTEST PEOPLE

Your ability to hire, train, and retain the very best people will be the difference between success and failure. That's true in a crisis and it is true when your business is taking off again. Never become complacent about seeking out the best and brightest people available. Skilled workers and smart leaders are always going to be in demand, no matter what the current unemployment level may be.

The hiring, training, and retention process is not something that gets in the way of your "real job"—it *is* your real job. Make no mistake: If you want to consistently grow your business, you need to out-hire the competition and do a better job of training and retaining the best and the brightest once they are in the fold. *Don't wait for growth before you hire the best and brightest. You hire the best and brightest to enable you to grow.*

SEEING THE FUTURE MORE CLEARLY

No one has the ability to predict the future. We do have the ability, however, to master the obvious. It's not easy to plan for the unexpected, but we can concentrate our thinking on a better understanding of the obvious trends affecting us. How they will they continue to impact our business in the future?

The human condition has changed drastically in the past 100 years, and the pace of change is only increasing. In order to grow, we need to see and understand the major trends taking place in the world today: the "grayification" of the populations of the western industrial nations; world populations on the move; an increasingly diversified U.S. consumer and workforce; China's impact on commodity prices and the dollar, just to name a few. These things already affect you. The question becomes, how will these obvious trends affect your future?

To more clearly see the future, you also have to look for the weak signals, too—those early indicators of change that are the first sign that things are shifting. Just as tsunamis start as a nearly imperceptible ripples that grow into powerful forces of change, so too can weak signals that are only in the periphery of our present view. Any leader who is attuned to these weak signals is far less likely to be caught off guard when the giant waves of change hit the shores. Growth comes from seeing these subtle waves of change more clearly and more quickly than others.

Companies that will experience the most profitable and sustainable growth will be those who have a 20/20 vision of the year 2020.

If you first duck and then look to recover, I believe you'll be in the best position to reap the rewards of an inevitable economic expansion. As you look for your opportunity, be sure to develop the following vital components:

- A mobilization effort that seeks to identify and fill new and changing markets.
- A strategy for partnering with other outstanding organizations that leads to a mutually beneficial relationship.
- An understanding of how to best evaluate the fit of a potential acquisition.
- A concerted effort to make use of the most efficient tools in your increasing sustainable business processes.
- An ongoing training investment in the great people who work with and for you.
- A system for how you allocate your time, money, and effort in order to lead a true growth company.

I started this book with a quote from one of my heroes, and I will end with him also. Mark Twain said, "I am an old man and I have known a great many troubles, but most of them never happened." I hope his words prove prophetic for you.

■ ■ ■

If you get a moment, please tell me how your duck and (re)cover plans are going at steven@stevenslittle.com.

Index

Index